Dedicated to:

To all my fellow sufferers...

Here's to making fewer trips to the E.R.

Coping Refined

The Anti-Anxiety Workbook

Written by Terry L Johnson

Coping Refined

The Anti-Anxiety Workbook

The most annoying statements that people can make when you are in the crux of a panic attack are, "Stop stressing," "Chill," or, "Just relax." If you could calm down, you would. However, as compared to the average person, the reality is that it takes a lot for you to calm down when having an anxiety attack. One who has suffered from anxiety, or, panic attacks, knows that relaxing is sometimes a task that requires work and effort.

Relaxation techniques should be used to supplement, and not replace, other CBT (Cognitive Behavior Therapy). Relaxation skills can be used to address the urgent need for the body to release symptomatic anxiety, by calming the mind, reducing muscle tension, and slowing down breathing. Relaxation techniques have a specific structure, for example, meditation, mindfulness, and diaphragmatic breathing.

Other methods, such as enjoying pleasurable activities and self-care, are helpful because they can help us feel relaxed. In this booklet, we will discuss some of these strategies to see why they work and how they can be best implemented. It is important to reiterate that relaxation techniques should be used together with other CBT methods and that they are most effective when consistently practiced.

Different strokes work for different folks, so find out the relaxation strategies that suit you.

Have fun!

What are Relaxation Exercises?

"Tension is who you think you should be. Relaxation is who you are." – Proverb

Robert sat in the train; heart rate elevated, palms sweaty, ears swooshing with the sound of his furiously pumping heart. He felt dizzy and leaned forward in his seat, desperately trying to calm the panic steadily rising in his mind.

Robert recognized the somatic or physical symptoms of the panic attack gradually taking over his body. He was now sweating profusely, in that cool winter atmosphere, he might as well have been on a tropical island. Robert started taking in deep exaggerated breaths, as he attempted to calm down his racing heart. His muscles felt tense; he balled up his fists and clenched his thighs and buttocks. Robert felt restless, keyed up, and "on edge." His concentration was off and his mind felt blurry. Early that morning he had woken up feeling perfectly fine and looking forward to the day. After all, he was on his way to his best friend's wedding!

The symptoms that Robert was feeling were a side effect of his body's attempts to protect him. His blood was moving around his brain and body, and into his large muscles, like his legs, arms, neck, and back, readying him to "fight" or to "flee." In other words, Robert's body was working hard to protect him, and the resultant feelings and sensations produced were uncomfortable.

Though it took him a few minutes of deep breathing and listening to music, Robert was eventually able to calm down. The relaxation techniques used by Robert on the train helped reverse his symptoms because his mind and body were forced into a space of not feeling the need to protect him.

Robert had experienced similar mild to extreme levels of anxiety for a long time, almost on a daily basis. He was constantly jittery and tense and had even forgotten what being relaxed felt like! His anxiety was "baseline" at a high level. That is until a Psychologist taught him how to practice relaxation techniques. On implementing the methods similar to those provided in this booklet, Robert was able to lower his panic/anxiety attacks, and he began to experience a measure of freedom that helped him regain his confidence.

Approach gaining relaxation skills just as you would exercise. If you were planning to enter into a 10K marathon race, it is reasonable for anyone to expect you to train for it. This expectation will only increase if you are a novice marathon runner. Your pre-marathon training schedule would consist of running at least 2 miles a day, over several weeks, steadily building up to 9 miles per day - that takes a considerable amount of discipline and dedication!

In the same manner, relaxation skills can only be developed over long periods. Obtaining relaxation techniques is not a one-time deal!

To get started, you may:

1. Fill in a self-care assessment questionnaire
2. Get relaxation exercises and practice them daily or several times a week. For example, mindfulness, progressive muscle relaxation (PMR), and deep breathing
3. Make your daily lifestyle less hectic, less busy or less rushed
4. Participate in activities that make you feel competent, give you pleasure, or help you break away from other stressful activities

Goals of relaxation techniques

1. Learn how and when to use the techniques
2. Learn how to breathe in ways that will promote relaxation and calm
3. Slow down your mind's activity and learn to tolerate better "racing thoughts"
4. Increase awareness of steadily rising tension in the body and be aware of the difference between relaxation and tension
5. Lower levels of restlessness and stress in the body
6. Incorporate daily/weekly activities that are fun and activities that make you feel competent
7. Learn to "slow-down" in your daily life by setting realistic goals and by purposing to have calmer days

The ultimate goal of relaxation strategies is, over time, to lower the body's levels of stress and anxiety.

Relaxation Strategies

In Cognitive Behavioral Therapy, relaxation strategies form part of a skill set. While we would all like to spend the better part of our day feeling good and relaxed, in the long run, relaxation skills alone will not improve our anxiety. An essential component of CBT is in knowing **why, how, and when** to implement certain techniques to identify which relaxation strategies are helpful or not.

To be clear, relaxation strategies should not replace exposure or cognitive skills. They should instead be used as a companion. The reason is that in the long run, relaxation strategies can actually make anxiety worse. Why you ask? Relaxation strategies are carried out during moments of distress as a way to ease anxiety. This, in turn, trains our brains to think of anxiety as a "bad." Therefore, every time anxiety presents itself, the mind will react by sending out stronger fear "alarms," leading to intense physical reactions to anxiety.

When to use relaxation strategies

- In daily practice, for example, exercise or meditation, will lower tension and over time, allow your body to feel calm
- During times of stress in order to function normally and to prevent the avoidance of integral life goals

Using relaxation strategies is assertive. For example, while doing an aerobic activity will not cure your anxiety, it'll help your brain realize that the concern is not dangerous, which will, in turn, make the stress more manageable

Good Attitude: "While doing this exercise will not cure me, it will help me have a good day and not avoid facing life."

When not to utilize relaxation strategies

- During times of severe distress or panic, to get rid of anxiety
- As a replacement for Cognitive Behavioral Therapy skills, e.g., exposure and cognitive restructuring

Why? The above two habits are "overprotective," and they train the mind to believe that anxiety is bad/dangerous, which in turn causes an increase in anxiety and somatic symptoms

Wrong Attitude: "I cannot stand this anxiety, it is unbearable, so I have to get rid of it now by doing something to make me feel better!"

How Should I Relax?

Everyone is different – one relaxation technique will benefit you, but not someone else. Perhaps there are methods that you already use to relax that work for you. Think about the activities, practices, or exercises that you regularly use to relax and list them below. Don't worry if you're having a hard time coming up with a list. By the end of this booklet, you should have a few ideas that you can put to use to achieve a calm mind.

1. _____

2. _____

3. _____

4. _____

5. _____

6. _____

7. _____

8. _____

9. _____

10. _____

Take home points:

Relaxation strategies are useful in reducing anxiety and stress levels over a duration of time. However, they are not a cure and are best used with other CBT techniques, e.g., exposure and cognitive restructuring.

Relaxation strategies should not be used to get rid of severe anxiety symptoms or panic attacks – they should be used to manage them. Each person should find their triggers and locate a set of skills and activities that may help them relax. Just like exercise, relaxation methods should be practiced regularly.

Breathe!

In the past, when facing a crisis or when feeling worried or upset about something, you may have been told, "Inhale deeply" or "Take a few deep breaths!" That's good advice because, on the one hand, altering your breathing may help you cool down if angry or slow down if frantic. Regulating your breathing by altering your breathing speed and intensity can change your body's anxiety response. In this section on breathing, you will learn how to develop correct breathing techniques, for example, slow diaphragmatic breathing, to communicate to your brain that you are safe.

Sometimes, depending on the intensity of the anxiety attack, breathing techniques may not be the best relaxation technique to use. However, breathing to slow down an increased heart rate caused by anxiety is an excellent way to quickly calm down the body and get through a difficult situation.

Learn the following exercise:

Slow Diaphragmatic Breathing

1. Mentally step back from what you are doing
2. While seated comfortably in an upright chair, feet flat on the floor, place your folded hands on your belly
3. Take in a deep breath, calmly and slowly. Don't breathe in exaggeratedly, take normal breaths. Your folded hands will move up as you inhale. Don't lift your shoulders as you breathe in, focus instead on gently filling up your stomach with air, without moving your shoulders
4. Breathe out slowly while counting to five. Reduce the volume and rate of the exhaled breath. On expelling the air from your lungs, hold your breath for 2-4 seconds or a max of 4 slow counts, before inhaling again
5. With repeated inhaling and exhaling, focus on slowing down the rate/pace of your breath
6. Practice this breathing technique for 10 minutes, at least twice a day. Make this breathing technique a lifestyle by finding regular time to practice it, each day

Tension Releasers

There are moments during the day when you can benefit from a time-out session. When you catch yourself yawning or sighing, it is time for a break because it's generally a sign that you aren't getting enough oxygen. Because a yawn or a sigh releases a bit of tension, you should practice yawning or sighing as a way to relax.

Make sure that you are standing straight when you do the following exercise:

Sighing:
1. Sigh deeply. As air rushes out of your lungs, release a sound of deep relief
2. Do not think as you inhale – let the intake of air be natural and effortless
3. Repeat several times until you feel relaxed

Yawning:
1. Open your mouth wide
2. Raise your arms and stretch them above your head
3. Yawn (exaggeratedly if possible)
4. Repeat as needed

Note: Be sure to step back mentally several times a day in order to check in with yourself. Ask yourself questions that will reveal your sense of relaxation at that point. For example, "Am I feeling any stress?" Nevertheless, you can get some tension release by simply breathing diaphragmatically a few times a day.

Breathing Tips:
1. The depth of the breath is less critical than the speed of the breath. Avoid "catching" your breath, which is caused by taking shallow breaths. Take deep and filling breaths
2. Breathing exercises are not meant to "eradicate" anxiety. They are instead designed to help you get through a difficult situation. Daily practice will help you "train" yourself to establish a "calm breathing" mindset over time
3. Practice, practice, practice! It takes time and effort to train the body to calm down via breathing techniques

Take home points:

Slow diaphragmatic breathing is a beneficial relaxation skill used by CBT practitioners and patients alike. Just like any exercise, it should be implemented frequently. For the best results, practice slow diaphragmatic breathing for 10 minutes per session, twice a day, daily.

Slow Down Your Mind

Mindfulness for relaxation and anxiety management

Observe the photo keenly and then do this exercise:

Describe what you see in objective terms only. Notice shapes, colors, shades, etc.

Write what you see in the provided space:

_____

_____

_____

_____

When looking at the above picture, what thoughts and memories come to mind? Let your mind wander and write whatever comes up, as soon it comes into your mind. Take 1-3 minutes to do this exercise.

_____

_____

_____

_____

This technique is referred to as mindfulness, and it originated from Buddhist meditation practices. Over the years, mindfulness skills have been studied and used in therapy by psychologists and physicians. Studies in the last 20 years or so show that mindfulness can alleviate anxiety and help patients calm their minds. So, how does mindfulness work?

Scientifically speaking, there isn't enough data that can provide proof as to why mindfulness is so effective. However, several theories explain its practical usage and helpfulness. The main focus and goal of mindfulness is to allow an individual to describe a variety of experiences non-judgmentally and objectively while focusing on the present moment.

It's a typical cognitive skill, in that it attempts to gather information and evidence around a thought that triggers anxiety, which in turn lessens the power and impact of that thought.

One way to lessen the magnitude of a thought is by seeing it for what it is: merely a thought. One wonderful attribute about thoughts is that they can change! Meaning that an oppressive and fear-mongering feeling can transform into an encouraging and hope-filled view. It is difficult to communicate the advantages of mindfulness, so how about trying to lesson below?

Mindfulness Exercise
1. Get comfortable. Lie down or sit upright with your feet on the floor. Begin by practicing slow breathing exercises to calm your mind. Focus your mind on your breathing. Think of how your breath flows into your nostrils and then out. Do this until you feel a sense of calmness

2. As you breathe, notice your minds tendency to wander. Now while still breathing deliberately, move from focusing on your breathing to concentrating on your mind. Your thoughts may wander to a memory, something that you are worried about, or plans for the day that you need to pursue. You may perhaps notice physical sensations in your body, for instance, an itch or pain. You may pick up a pleasant scent or unpleasant smell. Notice all these things and then return your mind and focus on deep breathing. Remind yourself that everything that you have thought about can be dealt with later. The present time is simply for focusing on your breathing and not what's on your mind. Pay attention to your breathing only, and nothing else

3. Your mind will wander after some time. Don't try to focus on any particular thing; simply focus on your breathing. When you notice that you are concentrating intensely on resolving a situation, simply return your focus to your breathing. This could take quite a bit of effort, but don't worry, focusing on your breathing will become second nature. Imagine that every passing thought, emotion or sensation – whatever it could be – is a floating cloud, gently moving in the sky, and which will be replaced by another one

4. Practice this mindfulness technique for 10 minutes. For best results, you may want to add time to your practice, e.g., 15 minutes instead of 10 minutes. Alternatively, you may increase the frequency of the practice, say, by training on mindfulness twice or thrice a day

5. There's no perfect way to practice mindfulness. The only thing that you need to be careful about is what you allow into your consciousness. Negativity and stressful thoughts are not permitted! When your mind wanders into negativity, work on focusing on your breathing only. It is impossible to go wrong with mindfulness – allow your mind to wander, and then focus on breathing

6. Use this mindfulness and relaxation audio to help you practice

Controlling Your Mind

In the chapter "Slow Down Your Mind," you learnt how to permit your mind to wander. Granted, this instruction is in conflict with most meditation or focus oriented exercises. In those exercises, one is usually instructed to allow something, for example, good thoughts to "control" their mind.

Research shows that the human mind cannot be controlled entirely. No matter how hard a person may try, they may find it very difficult to "control" their mind, especially when feeling anxious.

Why is this, you ask? Well, when a person is anxious, the amygdala, or the anxiety center of the brain, sends off an "anxiety alarm." It does this by alerting us to the possible presence of something harmful, either inside our bodies or in the environment. Think about it, if your mind is consumed by one task and only one task, you would become unaware of your environment, which would cause you to be open to danger! Therefore, the mind distracts you, in order to make you cognizant of your environment. This makes the mind very difficult to "control." Matter of fact, you may find that the more you try to control your mind, the more your mind works to distract you!

Reasons to Practice Mindfulness

Mindfulness is an essential part of CBT (Cognitive Behavioral Therapy) for the following reasons:

- Attempting to control the mind is an exercise in futility. Trying to control our thoughts actually makes us feel worse because we fail at it! The very first step in any CBT intervention is, "Don't control the mind by force." You'll only be able to manage anxiety with CBT techniques, once you grasp this truth

- Mindfulness helps us observe and recognize anxiety and other emotions, without needing to react to them. We instead learn to tolerate or accept these emotions, versus trying to eradicate them

- Mindfulness retrains the brain. Mindfulness helps the mind not react to anxiety, or rush to "fix" it, by communicating to the amygdala that the situation is not "dangerous." It trains the brain not to be unnecessarily fearful

- Stopping to pay attention to the present moment causes us to listen to our anxiety alarm. Mindfulness allows the mind to process the situation, and that prevents the mind from "fueling" the anxiety. In the long run, the mind and body learn that the "alarm' is unnecessary and can/should be turned off

Practice Becoming Mindful

Do this: pretend that your mind is a movie screen. You are seated in a beautiful movie theater, viewing what is being projected onto the large screen. You are not in control, so just watch and follow what you see.

Close your eyes and observe the thoughts, images, or memories being projected upon that screen. They may be random images or connected – whatever you view is fair game. If you start responding or feeling attached to the "movies" contents, acknowledge that attachment and then direct the "movie" playing in your mind to something else.

If it becomes too difficult to redirect your mind to other images or thoughts, practice the breathing techniques, and start over. Do this until you can manage, not control, your thoughts, and anxiety.

Take-Home Points

Mindfulness is a beneficial relaxation strategy because it calms the mind by reducing our desire to control it. Wanting to control the mind ultimately worsens anxiety. Mindfulness techniques focus on objective information about current experiences, including thoughts, emotions, sensations, and memories.

The aim of mindfulness in CBT is to teach people to notice various experiences without attempting to change them and without judgment. Mindfulness teaches a person to observe life experiences, just as one would watch images on a movie screen or clouds in the sky. Mindfulness techniques on their own cannot cure anxiety – they are instead used in conjunction with other CBT skills, and can provide an excellent foundation to develop those skills.

Meditation

Meditation is the practice of focusing on one thing. The object of meditation varies from one tradition to the next and may or may not be necessary, for example, sacred texts, inanimate or animate objects, etc. The meditator often repeats, either silently or aloud, a word, syllable, or group of words.

This is also known as mantra meditation. Focusing on an object such as a flower or a candle's flame can anchor one's attention. Most meditators find that a relaxing and convenient point of focus is their own breath. You can, however, use anything as your object of meditation, for example, the tip of your nose, your office calendar, or even a person's name.

It's crucial to comprehend that the core of meditation is not only about excluding all other thought but is also about the attempt to achieve this type of focus. The nature of the human mind is designed to be aware of its environment and possible dangers, making it difficult for people to sustain concentration over a long period. Numerous thoughts may appear and interfere with the meditation. A typical meditation might look as follows (in this case, the meditator has chosen to count to three repeatedly):

One .. two .. this isn't difficult .. one .. two .. three .. one .. I do not have any distracting thoughts at all .. oh, oh, that was a distracting thought .. let me start meditating .. one .. two.. three .. my nose itches .. one .. two .. I wonder where our anniversary dinner will be .. one .. two .. three.

In each instance, when the meditator realizes that her mind has drifted to other thoughts, she chooses to instead dwell on her meditation. By repeating this moment of awareness, a moment of noticing and then refocusing attention, over time, a couple of things may become apparent:

- It is impossible to fear, worry, or hate when one's mind is thinking about something apart from the object of these negative emotions
- You can choose the thoughts on which to dwell. You don't have to think about everything that comes to mind
- Your diverse thoughts fit into a few categories: fearful thoughts, grudging thoughts, angry thoughts, planning thoughts, wanting thoughts, memories, and so on
- Your behavior is based on beliefs that over a lifetime have become habitual. Patterns of perception and thought lose their influence over you, as soon as you become aware of them
- Emotions, aside from the images in your mind, consist entirely of your body's physical sensations
- The strongest feeling becomes manageable once you concentrate on your body's sensations versus the thought that caused the emotions
- Emotions and thoughts are not permanent. They move in and out of the mind and body – they need not leave any trace
- When you are mindful of life's "right now" occurrences, and are open to "what is," the extreme lows and highs of your emotional response to life will gradually disappear, and you will live your life with equanimity

In 1968, a test was conducted by Dr. Benson and Harvard Medical School to examine if meditation would counter the physiological effects of stress. Dr. Benson provided scientific proof that the physiological effects listed below were observed during meditation:

1. Heartbeat and breathing rates slowed down
2. Oxygen consumption fell by 20 percent
3. Blood lactate levels dropped (this level rises with fatigue and stress)

4. Skin resistance to electrical current, a sure sign of relaxation, increased fourfold

5. EEG ratings of brain-wave patterns indicated increased alpha activity, a sign of relaxation

Dr. Benson went on to provide proof that meditation could duplicate these physical changes if the following factors were present:

1. A moderately quiet environment
2. A comfortable position
3. A mental device that provides constant stimulus
4. A passive attitude

With regular meditation, a person can feel calmer and more focused in life, less prone to being reactive and more capable of speedy decision making,

SYMPTOM-RELIEF EFFECTIVENESS
Meditation has been used successfully to prevent and treat high blood pressure, migraine headaches, heart disease, and autoimmune diseases, for example, diabetes and arthritis. Meditation has proven helpful in curtailing anxiety, obsessive thinking, hostility, and depression.

TIME TO MASTER
The benefits of meditation only increase with practice, as levels of relaxation deepen. Attention becomes more focused, steadier. A person becomes more adept at living in the present. Therefore, it's important to meditate regularly.

INSTRUCTIONS
The following sections address the most important aspects of meditation: correct posture, practice time, and the need to center yourself.

Establishing Correct Posture
1. Select a comfortable position from the following:
   - Sit comfortably in a chair, legs uncrossed, knees apart, with your hands resting on your lap

- Cross-legged (tailor-fashion) on the floor. This position is most stable and comfortable when seated with a cushion under your buttocks. Both knees should be touching the floor
- Kneeling, with your heels, pointed outward and big toes touching. Your buttocks should rest comfortably on the soles of your feet. If you place a cushion under your buttocks and between your feet, to rest on, you'll be able to sustain the position for a longer duration (Japanese-fashion)
- The "full lotus" yoga position. This position is not recommended for beginners as it requires a lot of physical conditioning
2. Sit upright, but not ramrod rigid. With your back straight and your chin pulled in slightly, the weight of your head should rest directly on your spinal column. Arch the small of your back slightly
3. Briefly rock from side to side and front to back. In doing so, your upper torso should feel balanced on your hips
4. With your mouth closed, breathe through your nose. Press your tongue purposefully but gently against the roof of your mouth

Centering Yourself

Centering yourself or being centered means having and maintaining a place of calmness within yourself, through conscious thought and effort, regardless of the intensity of your churning emotions. Three steps to centering yourself are:

ESTABLISHING YOUR POSTURE

Japanese-fashion

Tailor-fashion

Yoga lotus position

GROUNDING

With your eyes closed, focus on the contact point between your body and the cushion or chair. What sensations do you feel? Next, pay attention to where your body touches itself. Are your hands or legs crossed? If they are, what is the sensation of the connecting points? Finally, focus on how your body occupies the space around you. Do you take up a lot of space? Can you discern the boundary between your body and the surrounding area? Notice your feelings.

BREATHING

Close your eyes and inhale deeply. Notice your breathing quality - is it slow or fast? Shallow or deep? Notice where your breath rests within your body. Is it high up in your chest, or is it around your stomach, in your midsection? Perhaps low in your belly? Move your breath from one area to another. Breathe in and fill your upper chest with air, and then breathe in filling up your stomach. Finally, fill up your lower belly.

Feel your lower abdomen as it expands and contracts, with air going in and out of it. Notice that your upper chest and stomach area appear to be still. This is the most relaxing stance to use while meditating; the "dropped breath." Don't worry if you aren't able to take deep belly breaths. As you practice meditation frequently, you will be able to master the dropped breath.

ATTITUDE

During meditation, the most important element in bringing about relaxation is having a passive attitude. As a beginner to meditation, you may struggle with having numerous thoughts and few instances of clear concentration. This is natural and to be expected. Your thoughts are important and integral to meditation – they are not interruptions. You wouldn't be able to release your thoughts if you didn't have them in the first place. An inability to comprehend your thoughts would hinder your ability to let go of, e.g., negative thoughts.

A passive attitude should not care about whether you are accomplishing things correctly, pursuing any goals, or even whether meditation is good for you. You should be able to have an attitude that thinks, "I'm going to spend my time sitting, meditating, and whatever happens, happens."

A WORD ABOUT TIME

In general, any time spent meditating will lead to relaxation. So, it's best to spend a bit of time meditating than not meditating at all. As a beginner, maintain a meditative posture only if it is comfortable. Don't push yourself; even five minutes a day is better than nothing. Forcing yourself to meditate may have you developing an aversion to meditation. As you practice, meditation becomes more natural, and you will find it easier to extend your meditation time and learn new positions. All you need is 20-30 minutes, once or twice a day, to achieve relaxation.

EXERCISES

The exercises below are divided into five groups:

- Group 1: Explains three basic meditations and their mechanics. Try each one a couple of times and then choose the one you like best. Practice at least once a day

- Group 2: Consists of meditation exercises which will help you relax your muscle groups at will

- Group 3: Introduces you to exercises in mindfulness. These exercises can be used anywhere to calm your body during stressful situations

- Group 4: Builds on the mindfulness techniques provided in Group 3. Living life will have you experiencing annoyances, pain, or disappointments, which can add up and cause you to become tense. By practicing meditation, you'll be able to handle life's irritations when they occur

- Group 5: Teaches you to release negative feelings and obsessive thoughts that make relaxation difficult, due to your mind wanting to hold onto, or rehash, an emotion or idea that you had experienced

Group 1: Three Basic Meditations

A. Mantra Meditation

Throughout the world, the mantra meditation is the most commonly practiced form of meditation. Before you begin, choose a syllable or word that pleases you. You may select a word that has significance to you, or nonsense syllables which are pleasant to utter. Dr. Benson recommends saying "one." Most meditators prefer saying "om."

Let's practice mantra meditation:

1. Find a comfortable posture, center yourself. Inhale slowly and deeply, several times
2. Chant your chosen mantra inaudibly. Within your mind, repeat the mantra over and over. When your thought strays, take note and then return your attention to the meditation. If you get uncomfortable or feel any sensation, e.g., itchy, pins and needles, take note, and then return your attention to the meditation – to your special word. Don't force it. Let your mantra develop its rhythm, as you think it repeatedly
3. You may want to chant your mantra aloud. Immerse yourself in the sound of your voice and relax. Do you feel more relaxed with an inaudible chant or an audible chant? Which is more relaxing?

4. Meditation refines your awareness and makes you become focused. If you feel that the mantra has become mechanical (sometimes sleep may take over, or you may become lost in thought), especially when inaudible, stay aware of each syllable.

B. Sitting Meditation

You begin sitting meditation by focusing on your breath.

Let's practice sitting meditation:

1. Choose a comfortable sitting posture
2. Focus on the soothing rise and fall of your breathing. Your breath is always there, just like ocean waves come to shore and then go back out. Focus on inhaling and exhaling, and the sensations from breathing in and out
3. With a wandering mind, let your breath anchor you to the present
4. When you become distracted by your thoughts, acknowledge and release them
5. "Name" the thoughts as you notice them. For example, if you notice that you are planning something, say to yourself quietly, "Planning, planning, I am planning." You can name reminiscing, planning, thinking, longing, or whatever is on your mind in the same manner: label it and move on. This will enable you to stop identifying and associating yourself with your thoughts. You will learn to let go to create peace and spaciousness.

This meditation takes 20-30 minutes to do. With frequent practice, you'll be able to let go of your thoughts more quickly, as you pay attention to your breathing

C. Breath-Counting Meditation

Breath-counting meditation is the alternative to sitting meditation. In this practice, you count the rhythm of the breath. Following the ins and outs of the breathing pattern creates a sense of rest and peace.

Let's practice breath-counting meditation:

1. Find a comfortable posture, center yourself. Inhale slowly and deeply, several times. Close your eyes. Alternatively, fix them on a spot four feet from you. You may or may not focus on an object

2. Take deep and comfortable belly breaths. Do not force the inhalation. As you do so, focus on each part of your breathing: inhaling, the turn (when you stop inhaling and start exhaling), exhaling, the pause (between exhaling and inhaling), the turn (when you start inhaling), and so on. Notice the pause. What are your physical sensations as you pause between breaths?
3. Say, "one" as you exhale. Continue counting each exhaled breath: "two .. three .. four." Then start again with "one." Start over if you lose count
4. When you discover wandering thoughts, note them and then return to counting your breath
5. If a particular physical sensation catches your attention, focus on it until it recedes. Return to inhaling, exhaling and counting your breath

SPECIAL CONSIDERATIONS
1. Becoming and feeling relaxed during meditation is a gradual process. Therefore, during the process of meditation, while you may feel restless and that your mind is wandering, at the end of the meditation, you will realize that you feel more relaxed than you felt before you began meditating
2. As your mind becomes quiet with meditation, hidden pain can materialize from the recesses of your subconscious mind. You may find that as you meditate that you feel depressed, angry, or frightened. Allow yourself to experience those thoughts and feelings without resisting them. Let go of the temptation to analyze or make sense of the emotions that you may experience. Talk to a friend, therapist, or meditation teacher if you need to
3. Meditation can and should be practiced in any environment, whether quiet or not. Life is seldom ideal, so don't let obstacles prevent you from meditating
4. Pick a regular place and time to meditate. Get a group of friends to practice meditation with you

Group 2: Releasing Muscular Tension

A. Body Scan or Inner Exploration
This exercise will enable you to focus on different parts of your body while noticing sensations and letting go of tension.

Let's practice a body scan:

1. Start by becoming aware of the rise and fall of the breath in your belly and chest. Ride the waves of your steady breathing and let it anchor you to the present

2. Focus on the soles of your feet. Notice any sensations without judgment. Be present with the feeling. After a few minutes, imagine that your breath is now flowing to the soles of your feet. As you breathe, you may experience a softening of tension. Observe carefully

3. Focus your attention on your ankles. Become aware of any sensation in that part of your body. Breathe into and out of your feet, while noticing the sensations

4. Proceed to all parts of your body in the same manner – knees, lower legs, pelvis, thighs, buttocks, and hips, upper and lower back, belly and chest, shoulders, neck, head, and face. Notice any difference in sensation in each body part, and let go of it as you move to the next part

5. Focus on any part that has tension, pain, or discomfort. Experience the sensations and relax. As you inhale and exhale, imagine the pain and tension flowing out of your body

6. When you reach the very top of your head, scan your entire body for areas of discomfort or tension. Imagine that you are breathing from a breath hole on your scalp, just like a whale or a dolphin. Breath from the top to the soles of your feet and through your entire body, repeatedly. Allow your breath to remove and wash away uncomfortable sensations or tension.

A complete body scan can take 20-30 minutes to do each day.

B. Moving Band Meditation

Let's do a moving band meditation:

1. Find your posture and center yourself. Take several deep breaths

2. Imagine that you have a three-inch band around the top of your head. Do you feel any tension in your forehead? If you do, try to relax. Are there any other sensations? Focus on them

3. Lower the imaginary band. Focus on the area taken up by the band. What does your eyeball feel like? The wall of your nose? Any tension? Try to relax. Breathe and whisper, 'Let it go. Let all tension go."

4. Move the imaginary bad lower down your body while focusing on sensations. When you notice tension, release it. As you do so, breathe and relax. Be aware of your muscles as they relax

5. The band is now on your torso. It goes around one arm, across your upper body, switches to the other arm, and across your back. Scan each arm and torso as though they were one unit. What

do the boundaries between your arms and the rest of your body feel like? Do you feel any tension in your shoulders or back? Anywhere else? Relax these areas

6. Move the band down to your legs, noticing and releasing any tension. Focus on the sensation of your feet on the floor.

This exercise can be experienced in two different ways. Try both choose the one which is relaxing for you:

1. Move the band down your body, slowly, experience each sensation, while noting the points of tension and releasing them
2. Lower the band quickly down your body. Give the area encompassed by the band a brief scan. Repeat this process several times in a row

Group 3: Mindfulness and Present-Moment Awareness

A good percentage of our stress is from thinking about the past and or worrying about the future. When living in the present, your attention is focused on the here and now, and there's no room for anything else – including anticipation of rejection or failure, regrets, or any stressful situation.

When in a meditative state, your attention should be focused on the object of meditation – inhale, exhale, or the quieting mantra that allows you to be in the present. Whenever thoughts of the past or future, aversions or desires, or anything else arises, take note of them, and calmly return your awareness to the present. Focusing on the present allows your mind and body to enter into relaxation.

Mindfulness meditation offers both insight and deep relaxation. It cultivates a harmonious relationship with what is, for example, nagging, uncomfortable feelings, obsessive thoughts, physical discomfort, or external stressors. By being open to your present internal experience, and not resisting it, you cultivate acceptance and the ability to rest in the present. In the first stage of the practice of mindfulness, present-moment awareness is cultivated by focusing on your breathing. Initial exercises may also include focusing on feelings, sounds, or body sensations. A mindful discipline such as tai chi, yoga, or qi qong may also help cultivate mindfulness.

Regardless of the object of focus, a nonjudgmental, gentle, and embracing attitude should be used to encounter everything that arises during your meditation. The stories a person tells themselves and their reaction to what is, causes a person's pain or suffering. Therefore, use low-level attention to notice negative thoughts without judgment, and then return to your object of focus.

If you start creating a story about it, e.g., my left knee is hurting, it'll never stop, notice the narrative and return to your breathing without getting trapped in your thoughts. Meditating like this trains you to encounter and manage internal or external stressors in your life. When you face stressors, don't allow yourself to go into habitual reactions, which only lead to suffering. Instead of getting stuck in reactivity, pause, breathe, and carefully choose your response. Make choices that bring about relaxation, connection with others, healthier thinking, health, insight, and more love.

Conscious-Eating Meditation

You eat every day. How often do you focus your attention on the food that you are eating while you eat it? Do you usually eat with friends, or in front of the television? While reading a book? Can you finish a three-course meal in ten minutes or less time?

Try the following conscious-eating mediation when alone. The food described, for the sake of having an example, is a cheese sandwich.

Let's do a conscious-eating meditation:

1. While sitting in front of your food, take several deep breaths. Notice the food's shape, color, and texture. Is it appealing? Are you able to restrain yourself from eating it? Take note of your feelings

2. Be aware of the fact that you intend to eat the sandwich. Slowly reach for the sandwich. Make a mental note of the action. Say to yourself, "Reaching .. reaching .." Labeling your actions helps you to stay aware. As you lift the sandwich, notice that motion of lifting by saying, "lifting .. lifting .."

3. As the sandwich nears your mouth, smell the food. What aromas do you recognize? How are you reacting to the aroma? Can you smell the mayonnaise? Is your mouth watering? Focus on the sensation of your body desiring the sandwich

4. As you bite into the sandwich, feel your teeth cut through the bread. When the bite is done, how is the morsel centered in your mouth? How is your tongue positioning the morsel so that it is between your teeth? Start chewing slowly. What sensations do your teeth feel? Your tongue? What flavors are you experiencing? The cheese? The tomato? How is your arm positioned as you chew? Is it placed on the table?

5. When you swallow, be aware of your contracting esophagus, relax as your food is pushed into your stomach. When you finish swallowing, focus on the location of the ingested food. Where is your stomach? Can you feel the sensations within your belly? Is your stomach empty or full? What size is it?

6. As you eat your sandwich, stay aware of all the sensations possible. Silently label each movement. Switch your eating hand so that the awkwardness may help you pay attention. As with any meditation, notice the present thoughts and then focus on the food

Walking Meditation

Most people walk miles during their daily routines, making walking a good opportunity. Focus on the act of walking in the same manner as focusing on your breath during sitting meditation. You can do walking meditation either indoors or outdoors.

Let's do a walking meditating:

1. Stand and relax your abdominal muscles. Inhale deeply. Feel your abdomen contract and expand with each breath. Start walking. As you walk, practice breathing from this relaxed position. As you walk, mentally repeat "in" as you inhale and "out" as you exhale

2. Walk in tandem with your breathing. Inhale when one foot touches the ground, exhale when the other touches the ground, without forcing your breathing. Observe the number of natural steps that you can take with each inhalation and exhalation

3. When wandering thoughts and images interrupt your focus, notice it and then return to breathing and walking

4. Pay attention to all walking sensations. Concentrate on your lower legs and feet. As you lift your legs, notice your muscles contract. Which part of your foot makes contact with the ground first? Shift your weight, moving from one foot to the other. What are the feelings in your knees and legs as they bend and straighten? Pay attention to the ground that you are walking on. Is its texture hard or soft? Do you notice any stones or cracks? In what ways does the sensation of walking on grass differ from walking on a pavement? Capture any wandering thoughts and let them go. Become aware of your present moment

5. An alternative method to walking meditation is to count your steps as you walk. For example, if taking three steps during inhalation and exhalation, say to yourself "In .. two .. three" and "Out .. two .. three" etc. Your inhaled breath may be shorter or longer than your exhaled breath and may

accommodate either fewer or more steps. Your step count may also vary from breath to breath. Pay attention to your breathing, and walking and adjust accordingly.

Seeing Meditation

Gazing meditatively at something, e.g., during a meeting, in a waiting room, or on a bus. Seeing meditation is a wonderful and inconspicuous meditation practice which can be done anywhere

Let's do a seeing meditation:

1. Find an object that you want to fix your eyes on. The object should be within your line of vision. Fix your eyes upon the object and take several belly breaths. Let it capture your attention. Focus on it as if it's the only object in the vicinity. Do not judge what you are looking at, or have thoughts about it. Just "see" the object. When random thoughts arise, make a note, and return to focusing on the object

2. Try using different objects. A few suggestions are:
   - Concrete objects - objects with a definite shape and size and shape, which are usually stationary
   - Natural objects - such as sand, the ocean, clouds, a pile of dry leaves, and so on
   - Vastness - any uniform and large surface such as a finely patterned rug, or carpet
   - Moving objects - cars on a busy street, a crowd of people, and so on. With objects of this nature, do not follow individual moving shapes with your eyes. Instead, focus on a point in space. Let all movement pass your field of vision.

Any simple activity can turn into meditation when you continuously apply your focus towards it. Another good mindfulness exercise is a daily activity, preferably a short one. All you'd need to do is concentrate on every action and sensation involving that activity. For guidance, use a strategy similar to the one provided in "Eating Meditation."

Therefore, you can practice concentrating when you brush your teeth, shave, fold clothes, wash dishes, or pull weeds. Note the thoughts that arise and the return to the task at hand with renewed concentration. While engaged in this activity, use your nondominant hand (though not while shaving). The resulting awkwardness will remind you to concentrate on the action.

Group 4: Mindfulness of Pain or Discomfort

As a general rule, people respond to irritation, pain, or any physical discomfort by either building a wall around it, trying to block off feelings, or implementing avoidance. However, when you resist pain, it hurts even more. So, when it hurts, even more, you will work that much harder to resist it. This creates a vicious cycle that produces one big knot of resistance and pain that is extremely difficult to undo.

The alternative approach is to try to soften around pain. This will require you to acknowledge the presence of pain in your life, and then allow yourself to experience whatever is hurting you, both physically and mentally. Be your own good nurse, tell yourself that it'll be well, hold your own hand, and observe yourself with compassion as you experience uncomfortable emotions and sensations. When you rest in the presence of an irritant, you consciously relax your clenched muscles; you become able to focus on the hurt itself, without the tension that you would otherwise add to it.

Softening means that you pay attention to discomfort while disregarding your thoughts about how awful the discomfort is, how you cannot stand it, how you have to scratch, how you have to move, and so on. Softening can be likened to removing hard lumps and stones out of clay so that you can have a smooth and workable mound of clay. It is like thawing out meat so that you can cut out the bone. It's like cleaning the grime off a window so that you can peer into a room and see more clearly.

The following exercise introduces simple irritations into your basic meditation. By training in a safe setting, you will begin understanding the softening process.

Let's practice mindfulness of pain and or discomfort:
1. Find a comfortable posture and center yourself. Inhale slowly, deeply and severally, for a few minutes
2. Decide within yourself that for a predetermined amount of time, e.g., 10 minutes, you will not move. Set the alarm or timer and begin your meditation
3. You may get uncomfortable and shift in your seat without realizing it. This is fine. Notice the movement and resume your meditation. After a couple of practice sessions, you will notice your intention to move any part of your body before you do so

4. Once you learn how to identify your intention to adjust your physical position, try to focus on what your desire is. Do you want to stretch your back muscles? Squirm around in your chair? Maybe an ant is crawling on your arm, or you have an itch. Try to identify the uncomfortable sensation. With that said, be careful not to move

5. Try to focus on the discomfort. Relax any tight muscle groups. Check those muscles often, because with every uncomfortable thought they'll not stay relaxed. Check your breathing. Is your breath high in your chest? If it is, drop your breath into your belly. What is the current feeling? Focus on any sensation of discomfort and stay with it for a few minutes

6. When time is up, sit or lay down in any comfortable position. Focus on the sensations. In what way have the sensations improved? Does your body feel better, less tense? Is the relief immediate or gradual? If there's any tension, release it.

Any irritation, be it sound or sensation, can be used in meditation as a focal point. Focusing on minor body aches, the sound of a dog barking, or a lawnmower, can teach you how your mind and body respond to life's irritations. Once you realize this, you'll be able to learn how to soften when you encounter such irritations

Group 5: Letting Go of Thoughts

Many cultures practice this highly structured exercise. In this practice, you passively observe your feelings, perceptions, and the flow of your thoughts, one after the other, without being concerned about their meaning or their relationship. This will enable you to see what is occupying your mind so that you can let it go.

Let's practice letting go:

1. Find a comfortable posture and center yourself. Inhale slowly, deeply and severally, for a few minutes

2. Close your eyes. Imagine that you are sitting at the bottom of a very deep pool of water. When you have a feeling, thought, or perception, imagine that it is a bubble and let it float away from you and disappear. When that thought or feeling is gone, another thought will appear and you will repeat the process. Don't think about the bubble's contents. Just observe it lift up from you, and float away. Sometimes the same bubble may show up numerous times, or several bubbles will appear to be interconnected. That's okay. Don't focus on them; just let them away from you.

3. If you feel uncomfortable about being "underwater" in your imagination, imagine instead that you are seated at a riverbank, watching a leaf gently drift downstream. Imagine one feeling, thought, or perception as the leaf. Let that leaf and therefore thought, drift out of sight. Look out at the river, and wait for another leaf (thought) to float by.

If you prefer, imagine your thoughts as puffs of campfire smoke and let them lift off from you. Meditation can bring a sense of renewal, insight, and focus to your life. Give yourself the benefit and gift of meditation.

Progressive Muscle Relaxation

Relaxation is sometimes considered to be the "absence of tension in the muscles." Imagine being able to release all the tension in your body without needing medication or alcohol!

A Chicago physician in the 1920's, Dr. Edmund Jacobson, purposed to do just that when he created a set of exercises that promised to ease muscle tension. His book entitled Progressive Relaxation promised to help people achieve relaxation through physical training. Dr. Jacobson was aware that our body's anxiety response was incompatible with deep muscle relaxation. He proposed that by consciously reducing muscle tension, people could reduce how anxious they felt.

The main goal of what we now refer to as Progressive Muscle Relaxation (PMR) is to learn how to release muscle tension through daily exercise. This daily practice communicates safety and calm to the mind and body, therefore reducing the brains' need to activate the anxiety alarm, aka, the "flight or fight" response.

<u>**Example: PMR Exercise**</u>

To do this PMR exercise, tense the muscles of your arms by "flexing" your biceps (see picture below). Hold that tense bicep position until you feel significant tension or 5-7 seconds

Now release by dropping your arm – let your arms rest. Pay attention to the tension that you felt when your bicep was flexed and compare it to the relaxed sensation taking over your arm. Focus on the feeling of warmth as blood flows to your arm. PMR can be conducted on any muscle group in the body as a regular exercise and becomes even more effective over a period.

PROGRESSIVE MUSCLE RELAXATION: SYMPTOM-RELIEF EXERCISES
Progressive Muscle Relaxation has been found to alleviate muscular tension, depression, anxiety, insomnia, fatigue, high blood pressure, neck and back pain, stuttering, and mild phobias.

TIME TO MASTER
To master PMR, practice the following PMR movements in fifteen-minute sessions, for one to two weeks, twice a day.

To start, you can use the available "<u>Progressive Muscular Relaxation</u>" track. The track runs for about 16 minutes in duration, and it will help relax your body as it moves from one muscle group to another. You'll achieve the best results by practicing PMR techniques twice a day, morning and evening.

INSTRUCTIONS

Most people don't know which of their muscle groups is chronically tense. When you practice PMR, you focus on the sense of tension in one precise muscle group at a time. When you release that tension, also focus on the sense of relaxation in that muscle group. Move progressively through your entire body, from one muscle group to the next. Repeat this procedure. By using the provided PMR techniques below, you will learn to distinguish between deep relaxation and tension.

PMR can be practiced either seated on a chair or lying down. Each muscle group should be tensed from 5-10 seconds and then relaxed for 20-30 seconds. You can adjust the timing according to your preference. If you find it challenging to bring a muscle group to the point of relaxation, practice by tensing and releasing it.

Once you get comfortable with the procedure, close your eyes, and focus on one muscle group at a time. It would be helpful to record the written instructions below, or purchase a professional recording such as **Fanning and Matthew McKay's Progressive Relaxation and Breathing** audio CD guide.

The following PMR instructions are divided into two sections. Part one deals with the basic procedure. You may want to record and replay part one while practicing. This will enable you to familiarize yourself with the muscle groups in your body that are often tense. If you use a recording, be sure to pause for tensing and relaxing – don't rush through the instructions.

Section two is a shorter procedure that simultaneously tenses and relaxes many muscles at a go. Therefore, deep muscle relaxation can be achieved with minimal time and effort.

Three Basic Levels of Tensing

There are three basic levels that you can use when practicing progressive muscle relaxation. With experience, you will be able to decide which level of tensing meets your needs. The movements below are effective and should be pleasant and not uncomfortable.

1. Active Tensing

   This involves tensing a muscle group very tightly, without hurting yourself. Study the sensations of tension, release the tension, and study the sensations of relaxation in that particular area. When tensing one muscle group, the rest of your body should be relaxed. Remember to breathe diaphragmatically even when tensing. Don't hold your breath.

   By exaggerating the tension, you will feel where you endure chronic tension; the tense spot may feel sore to the touch. For those that do not have any injuries and who do not contact extremely tense, active tensing should be the chosen PMR method, for the first time you do PMR.

   Regardless, most people use this preferred level every time they practice PMR. This is because tensing the muscles fatigues all the muscle fibers while releasing the tension feels pleasant and very relaxing. The sensation is similar to setting down hefty bags that you have been holding for a duration while queuing.

2. Threshold Tensing

   It is similar to active tensing except that particular muscle groups are tensed very slightly. This tension is barely noticeable to one observing. Threshold tensing should be used by those who have mild injuries, or who are very tense, to avoid injury or pain.

   Most people prefer threshold tensing once they've mastered the basic muscle groups via active tensing. Threshold tensing feels less invasive and requires less effort, so some people threshold tensing from the jump, due to extreme tension or health issues.

3. Passive Tensing

   Passive tensing is similar to active tensing except that with the "tensing phase," you notice any (slight) tension present in a specific muscle group. If no sensation is felt, you may do threshold tensing. Passive tensing should be used once you've familiarized yourself with threshold and active tensing. A round of relaxation using passive tensing, following a series of either threshold or active tensing, may deepen your state of relaxation.

VERBAL SUGGESTIONS

As you release the tension in a muscle group, you may find it helpful to say one or more of the expressions below:

Calm and rested.

Deeper and deeper.

Let go more and more.

Let go of the tension.

Let the tension dissolve away.

Relax, smooth out all the muscles.

Progressive Muscle Relaxation Script - Basic Procedure

1. To avoid being disturbed or interruption, select a quiet room. Get into a comfortable position

2. Remove your shoes and loosen your clothing. Loosen or remove any restrictive items, e.g., ties, Spanx etc

3. Take a few deep breaths, slowly, and begin to relax

4. As you let your entire body relax, clench your fists and gently bend them backward at the wrist

5. Tighter and tighter, clench on

6. Feel the tension in your forearms and fists

7. Now relax

8. Feel the looseness in your forearms and hands. Notice the difference in sensation, contrasted with the previous tension

9. Repeat all the above one more time, if you have the time

10. Bend your elbows and gently tense your biceps. Gradually tense them as much/hard as you can, while observing the feeling of tautness

11. Drop your hands to your sides and relax. Feel the difference

12. Focus on your head and face. Tightly wrinkle your forehead. Feel the tension in both your scalp and forehead

13. Relax your forehead and smooth it out. Imagine your entire scalp and forehead at rest and becoming smooth

14. Now frown intensely and notice the strain spreading across your forehead. Release. Smoothen out your brow

15. Squeeze your eyes closed gently, now tighter. Relax your eyes

16. Let your eyes remain closed, comfortably and smoothly. Open your mouth slightly, now open wide and focus on the tension in your jaw

17. Relax your jaw. Ensure that your lips are relaxed. Notice the marked difference in sensation between tension and relaxation

18. Press your tongue with force, against the roof of your mouth. Note the strain in the roof and back of your mouth. Relax

19. Press your lips and then purse them into an "O." Relax your lips. Feel the relaxation on your forehead, eyes, scalp, jaw, lips, and tongue. Let go even more. Allow the sense of relaxation to take over

20. Now roll your head, slowly tilt your head forward, to the side, back, to the side and forward, in a smooth 360-degree rotation. Now, in the opposite direction, make the same motion

21. Relax and return your head to a comfortable upright position

22. Now shrug your shoulders and lift your shoulders towards your ears. Hold that position. Drop your shoulders and feel the relaxation spread through your throat, neck, and shoulders. Feel pure relaxation taking over

23. Breathe in deeply and fill your lungs completely. Now hold your breath and experience the tension. Now exhale and allow your chest to relax/become loose

24. Continue relaxing, and let your breath come gently and freely. Notice the tension leaving your muscles with each exhaled breath

25. Next, tighten your stomach. Hold the position and feel the pressure. Relax

26. Now place one hand gently on your stomach. Breathe in deeply, filling your belly with air and causing it to push your hand up. Hold and then relax. As the air rushes out, observe the sense of relaxation taking over your body.

27. Now without straining, arch your back. Have the rest of your body in a relaxed position

28. Focus on the tension located in the lower part of you back. Relax. Let the tension dissolve away. Clench/tighten your thighs and buttocks. Relax and feel the difference. Straighten and tense your legs, while also curling your toes downward

29. Feel the tension. Relax. Straighten and also tense your legs while bending your toes towards you. Relax. Feel the heaviness and warmth of deep relaxation taking over your body, even as you breathe deeply and slowly. Relax as you let go of every bit of tension in your body

30. Relax your feet and your ankles; relax your calves and your shins; relax your knees and your thighs. Relax your buttocks

31. Feel the relaxation as it spreads to your stomach, and your lower back, your chest. Let go and let the sense of relaxation take over, even up to your shoulders, arms, and hands

32. Notice the feeling of relaxation and looseness in your scalp, face, jaw, and your neck. Breathe deeply and slowly

33. Your body should now be comfortable, relaxed, calm and rested

Shorthand Procedure

Once you've mastered the basic process, use the following steps to quicken the muscle relaxation process. In the procedure below, whole muscle groups are tensed simultaneously and then relaxed. As previously stated, for best results, repeat each procedure once, while tensing each muscle group for 5-7 seconds and then relaxing for 20-30 seconds.

Pay attention to the contrasting sensations between tension and relaxation:

1. Curl both fists and tighten your biceps and forearms (the Charles Atlas pose). Relax
2. In a clockwise direction, roll your head around. Now reverse. Relax
3. Like a walnut, wrinkle the muscles of your face: eyes squinted, shoulders hunched, mouth opened, and forehead wrinkled. Relax
4. Take a deep breath, fill up your chest with the air, and arch your shoulders back as you do so. Hold. Relax. Take another deep breath while pushing out your stomach. Hold. Relax
5. Straighten and also tense your legs while bending your toes towards you. Tighten your shins. Hold. Relax. Straighten and tense your legs while also curling your toes downward and simultaneously tightening your calves, buttocks, and thighs. Relax

On mastering the PMR techniques, you may want to try Applied Relaxation, which is described in the next section. Applied Relaxation builds on the lessons learnt in PMR and helps us learn to relax at a much faster rate.

Applied Relaxation

Swedish physician Dr. L.G. Öst developed Applied Relaxation from Progressive Muscle Relaxation principles. This set of skills allows you to relax quickly. Applied Relaxation takes time to develop, as seen from the outline below. Each treatment stage requires one to two weeks of practice.

Applied relaxation is the redacted version of progressive muscle relaxation. It teaches patients to react less strongly to their anxiety symptoms. AR therapy is taught to patients as a skill, just like riding a bike or driving a car, in order to master the skill of relaxation without needing a typical relaxation setting, for example, a quiet room.

The ultimate aim of AR therapy is to help the patient relax quickly and overcome physical symptoms of phobia and anxiety before they are intensified by the subjective and psychological symptoms which follow them.

The two main prongs of Applied Relaxation treatment are:

a)   teaching the patient how to recognize oncoming anxiety symptoms

b)   teaching the patient how to alleviate and deal with anxiety, without becoming overwhelmed by it

Firstly, patients who suffer from anxiety are advised to look out for signals that indicate oncoming stress, with self-observation at home, outside a therapeutic setting. The patients are provided with "worksheets" on which to record anxiety related symptoms, over a couple of weeks.

The first actual phase or AR therapy involves **PMR techniques** that focus on relaxing the neck, face, shoulders, hands, and arms. In a second session, the focus is on the relaxation of the chest, back, midriff, legs and feet.

Start by tensing each of the listed muscle groups for five seconds each, i.e., first the face, neck, shoulders, and finally, the arms and hands. Follow that with 15 seconds each, focusing on relaxing each muscle group. The second set of muscle group relaxation focuses on the chest, back, midriff, legs and feet. The aim is to relax the entire body while tensing a specific muscle group. At the conclusion, the individual should record the level of their overall tension, i.e., 0%, 50%, or 100%.

The **release-only** phase is the second phase of AR therapy. The release-only stage reduces relaxation time. This practice phase lasts one to two weeks. With release-only, the therapist encourages relaxation by focusing on breathing, relaxing face muscles of the head and face, progressively moving down the body until finally reaching the toes. In this stage, the focus is removed from tensing and relaxing the different muscle groups. However, this is not a hard and fast rule and should be adjusted according to the patients' need for relaxation in a particular area.

The next phase is **cue-controlled relaxation**. In this phase, both inhalation and exhalation are focused on, and verbal cues are also used to initiate relaxation more speedily. The verbal cue most commonly used is "relax."

The patient first reaches relaxation via the release-only method, and the patient indicates this to the therapist by raising their index finger. Thereafter, the patient is asked to focus on their breathing. Prior to each inhalation, the therapist says the word "inhale," and before each exhalation, the therapist says the word "relax." The therapist stops giving verbal cues, and the patient is instructed to use thought prompts by thinking "inhale" (inhalation) and "relax" (exhalation).
After a few minutes of thought prompts, the therapist verbally instructs using the cues "inhale" and "relax," five times, and then the patient resumes with the thought prompts. This entire session is repeated after a 15-minute break. After one-two weeks of practice, the patient should be able to reach relaxation much faster.

The **differential phase** of applied relaxation aims to teach the person how to relax in stress-inducing or normal situations, for example, in day to day life. The individual is taught to use cue-controlled relaxation when standing or seated upright, and to get to relaxation while moving about, or walking.

Rapid relaxation uses various cues to remind the individual to self-induce relaxation, such as whenever he/she looks at a watch or closes or opens a door. This form of relaxation uses the cue-controlled method – taking three to four deep breaths while thinking "relax" (exhalation). The focus is learning to use cue-controlled relaxation just before exposure to an anxiety producing trigger, and during and after exposure to a trigger. Cue-controlled relaxation is utilized as a means of coping with and reducing the adverse effects of anxiety.

Finally, patients are encouraged to use **applied relaxation** daily, whether they experience an anxiety attack or not, in order to maintain the ability to deal with it quickly and effectively.

Release-only Relaxation Script

As the name suggests, release-only relaxation removes the first step in PMR: the tensing step. This means you can achieve deep relaxation in half the time. With practice, mental focus is sufficient for draining the tension from your muscles, without needing to tense them first. This skill depends entirely on your ability to tell the difference between deeply relaxed and clenched muscles.

Before beginning the following release-only exercises, be sure to be proficient in progressive muscle relaxation:

A. Sit upright in a comfortable chair, arms at your side. Make sure that you are comfortable by moving around a bit

B. Focus on your breathing. Inhale deeply and savor the air filling your stomach, lower chest, and upper chest. Hold your breath for three seconds, sit up straight, and exhale through your mouth – feel the worry and tension leave your body in the exhaled stream of breath. On completely exhaling, relax your chest and stomach. Continue the process by taking full, calm and even breaths – notice the sense of relaxation taking over your body, with each breath

C. Relax your forehead, smooth out all the worry lines. Breath deeply, now relax your eyebrows. Let the tension melt away, down to your jaw. Release all your stress. Now open your mouth and relax your tongue. Inhale and exhale, while relaxing your throat. Notice how relaxed your entire face feels

D. Roll your head gently, clockwise. Feel your neck relax. Rest your shoulders; let them drop. Your neck is relaxed and your shoulders are low and heavy. Let that sense of rest flow through your arms to your fingertips. Your arms should feel loose and heavy. Your mouth should remain open, and your jaw feel relaxed

E. Inhale deeply, feel your chest expand, and your stomach too. Hold your breath and then exhale slowly in a smooth and steady stream through your mouth

F. Feel the muscles in your abdomen release tension and assume its natural shape. Relax both your back and waist. Breathe deeply, while noticing how heavy and loose your upper body feels

G. Now relax the lower part of your body. Feel your buttocks resting on the chair. Relax your thighs and knees. Feel the relaxation flow through your calves to your ankles, the bottoms of your feet, down to the tips of your toes. Your feet should feel heavy and warm as they rest on the floor. With each breath, feel your relaxation deepen

H. As you continue to take moderately deep breaths, scan your body for tension. Your back and legs are relaxed. Your face, arms, and shoulders are relaxed. You should be experiencing a feeling of warmth, peace, and relaxation

I. If any of your muscles still feel tense, turn your attention to the muscle group. Is it your shoulders, back, thighs, or jaw? Focus on the specific muscle and tense it. Clench it tightly and then release it. Feel it become as relaxed as the rest of your body - in deep relaxation.

The instructions for release-only relaxation may appear simpler than those for PMR. However, the processes involved are more complex. Be careful to drain the tension from each muscle you focus on. You should feel as relaxed as with the PMR routine. Don't force the relaxation; it will become easier to feel well-rested.

To master release-only relaxation, you will need a one to two weeks session. When you are able to relax in one five – seven-minute session, you are ready to move on to step three.

Cue-controlled Relaxation Script

Cue-controlled relaxation reduces relaxation time to two or three minutes. This stage focuses on your breathing, and it conditions you to relax on cue; that is, exactly when you instruct yourself to relax. The following instructions will help you build associations between cues, e.g., the command "relax" and true muscle relaxation.

Make sure that you are comfortable with release-only relaxation before you begin the following exercises:

A. Sit comfortably in a chair, arms at your side, and feet flat on the ground. Inhale deeply and hold for a moment. Exhale via your mouth in a smooth stream. Empty your lungs and feel your chest and stomach relax

B. Begin to relax from your forehead to your toes, using the release-only technique. See if you can relax completely in 30 seconds. If you need more time to get to relaxation, that's fine

C. You should feel peaceful and at ease. Your chest and stomach are moving, with slow and even breaths. The sense of relaxation intensifies with each breath

D. Breathe deeply and regularly, while saying "breathe in" as you inhale and "relax" as you exhale. Each breath brings peace and calm in, even as worry and tension dissipate

E. After a few minutes, stop saying, "breathe in" and "relax." If playing a recording with instructions, pause the recording. Focus your attention on the words "breathe in" and "relax" as relayed inaudibly in your mind. Close your eyes if it will help you focus more on the mental instructions. Relax

F. Now speak the words audibly as you breathe in deeply. Start feeling relaxed

G. Continue breathing while mentally saying the words for a few more minutes. Feel each breath bring calm and peace and dissipate stress (stop any recording and rest)

H. Repeat the cue-controlled relaxation process once more, after ten to fifteen minutes of rest

Be sure to be able to relax completely within two to three minutes before practicing rapid relaxation.

Rapid Relaxation Script

Rapid relaxation reduced relaxation time to less than thirty seconds. During incidences of severe panic and situations that introduce high levels of stress, you will have to be able to get urgent relief very quickly. Choose something that you frequently see throughout the day, for example, a picture frame that you see as you have your meals. If you can, put a "special cue" mark with a piece of colored cello tape while you practice this technique.

When ready to begin, look at your cue. Inhale and relax. Inhale and relax. Look at the colored cue, continue inhaling and exhaling slowly, and think "relax." Inhale and relax. Breath deeply and evenly, even as you continue to think "relax" every time you exhale. Allow the sense of relaxation to take over your mind and body permission.

Scan your body for tension, try to relax any muscle not required for the activity you are currently doing. Throughout the day, practice these simple steps as you look at your cue:

A.   Take two to three deep and even breaths. Exhale through your mouth

B.   Every time you exhale, think "relax" and continue to breathe deeply

C.   Scan your body for tension. Focus on the muscles that need release from tension. Relax

Use your relaxation cue at least fifteen times a day so as to relax quickly during natural, non-stressful situations. This routine will instill a habit of checking for tension and pursuing a state of deep relaxation daily. After the first couple of days, change the color of the cue cello tape or change the cue altogether. This will have the idea of relaxation constantly fresh in your mind.

Finally, use rapid relaxation to calm yourself in the instance that you have a particularly stressful day. The next stage is applied relaxation, which will help you refine your ability to relax.

Applied Relaxation Script

This is the final stage of AR training. It involves relaxing quickly when facing anxiety provoking moments. You will use the same method practiced in rapid relaxation, by beginning the deep breathing process the moment you notice a reaction to stress setting in. If you are not aware of your body's unique stress warning signs, for example, sweating, rapid breathing, or an increased heart rate, fill in the workbooks below to think through and find out your triggers and emotional responses. Also ask friends who have observed you in a stressful situation, to give you their input. The sooner you can identify your physiological response to stress, the more effectively you can apply the remedies provided in this booklet. Cut in on stress before it builds up and manifests forcefully.

As soon as you observe signs of stress – if you feel a flush of heat, catch your breath, or feel your heart leap – begin your three steps:

A.   Take three deep and even breaths

B.   Think these calming words, as you continue to breathe: Breathe in and relax .. Breathe in and relax. You may also prefer to think "relax" every time you exhale

C.   Scan your body for tension, focus on relaxing the muscles you don't need to use at that point

For example, if you are at your office desk, you can consciously relax your head, abdomen, and the lower part of your body. The muscles in your eyes, neck, chest, back, shoulders, arms, and hands can remain tense so that you can type on the keyboard and look at your computer monitor.

To reproduce the feeling of a stress reaction, complete some jumping jacks, or run up a flight of stairs and then practice these instructions. When you feel even more confident, visualize a stressful situation, e.g., an unpleasant encounter with your boss, or a fight with your spouse.

Practice makes perfect. So, prepare for that stressful situation so that it doesn't overwhelm you when it does materialize. Be patient with yourself and consider the benefits that will be enjoyed by all when you master your responses to stressful situations.

Full scripts and audio are available in the Davis, Robbins, and McKay's Relaxation and Stress Reduction Workbook and Fanning and Matthew McKay's Progressive Relaxation and Breathing and Applied Relaxation Training (Relaxation & Stress Reduction Audio Series) 1st Edition

Summary:

Gradually quicken your progress and overall relaxation time, by following the steps below:

1A: Progressive Muscle Relaxation (Basic Procedure)

Do a **Progressive Muscle Relaxation (PMR)** exercise while guided by a recording. PMR causes you to be aware of your muscles when in a tense state and when relaxed. Practice tensing and relaxing individual muscle groups, in the morning and in the evening, for at least two weeks.

Get started with the Progressive Muscle Relaxation script provided above, or the audios provided below. The exercises will help relax your body as you move from one muscle group to another. You'll achieve the best results by practicing PMR techniques once or twice a day, morning and or evening

Video: Progressive Muscle Relaxation - 17 Muscle Groups - Beginner Status 27 mins

Video: Progressive Muscle Relaxation Basic Procedure 15 mins

App: Progressive Muscle Relaxation - PMR Pro - English

1B: PMR, Shorthand Procedure

Once you have mastered the basics of PMR (Progressive Muscle Relaxation), learn to reach a relaxed state faster by exercising larger groups of muscles at the same time. This will reduce PMR exercise time to 6-8 minutes.

Video: How to do Progressive Muscle Relaxation 6 mins

2. Release-Only Relaxation

In this phase of the Applied Relaxation treatment, the "tensing" step is omitted in order to focus on learning how to release muscles and feel relaxed quicker, in 5-7 minutes

3. Cue-Controlled Relaxation

Cue-Controlled Relaxation reduces the total amount of time needed to achieve deep relaxation. For example, when we say "relax," we are able to relax instantly. In most cases, this enables one to reduce the time to achieve relaxation to around 2-3 minutes.

4. Differential Relaxation

This exercise helps you relax, even while conducting daily activities. Most activities involve the use of certain muscle groups, but some don't. This step enables you to isolate the specific muscle groups needed for a particular task while allowing the rest of your body to rest. This allows us to incorporate relaxation in our daily activities

5. Rapid Relaxation

Rapid Relaxation enables us to reduce relaxation time down to 20-30 seconds. In this step, we learn to pick an item in our daily life which we can access easily and regularly, for example, a watch or clock, and associate this cue with the relaxation skills taught in previous stages. It may be helpful to put colored tape on the cue of your choice. Practice this technique daily, 15-20 times a day, during situations that are normal and not stressful. You'll be ready to move to the next step when you can experience relaxation within 20-30 seconds

SPECIAL CONSIDERATIONS

1. If making a recording of the above procedures, space each instruction so that enough time is provided to be able to experience tension and relaxation before moving on the next muscle group
2. Practice while seated in an upright position as the position represents a typical public environment
3. Practice regularly to enhance the speed, depth, and intensity of your relaxation
4. Be careful when tensing your back and neck, because excess tightening can cause muscle or spinal damage. Overtightening of your feet and toes can result in muscle cramping
5. Don't release tension gradually. The correct technique is to release/relax/let go instantly; allow your muscles to become limp suddenly
6. While the instructions call for a quiet place to practice in. These methods are to be used whenever and wherever. Use the shortened version anywhere. These exercises should be implemented even in a public place, whenever you feel you need them

Take-Home Points

Progressive Muscle Relaxation (PMR) exercises help us reduce tension and anxiety in the body. Through practice, by tensing and relaxing different muscle groups in the body, you learn the difference in sensation between a relaxed muscle and a tense muscle. This will help you recognize the instances when you are tense and will, therefore, allow you to release muscle tension. Relaxation takes time to master, so practice regularly!

Applied Relaxation allows you to reach a relaxed state much faster, even under stressful circumstances, by combining it with PMR skills

Visualization

In this chapter on visualization, you will learn to:

- Manage stress-related conditions
- Tap into your imagination to relax
- Create a relaxing and safe place in your mind

BACKGROUND

Your imagination is a powerful tool that you can tap into to significantly reduce stress. The practice and power of positive thinking to treat physiological symptoms was first popularized by French pharmacist, Emil Coué, in the nineteenth century. Emil believed that the imagination is a powerful force that far exceeds the will. It is difficult to will yourself into a relaxed state, but you can use your imagination to sense relaxation spreading through your body, and you can travel in your mind and visualize a safe and beautiful refuge.

Coué taught that a person's thoughts become reality. In essence, you are what you think. For example, if you entertain sad thoughts, you will feel unhappy. If you dapple in anxious thoughts, you become tense. In order to overcome the sense of tension or unhappiness, you can redirect your mind to think of positive and healing images. When you predict that you will probably be miserable and lonely, for whatever reason, your prediction may come true. This is because any negative thoughts you may have will be exhibited in your social behavior. A person who claims that they'll get a stomachache or headache if the boss yells at them will likely have those thoughts take on a somatic form.

Coué found that diseases such as tuberculosis, fibrous tumors, constipation, and hemorrhages were often worsened when a patient focused on them. Therefore, his patients were instructed to say aloud, upon awakening, and at least 20 times a day, the famous phrase, "Every day in every way I am getting better and better."

Coué also taught his patients to practice general relaxation of their muscles before they retired to bed. He encouraged them to get into a relaxed and comfortable position and close their eyes. As they started to drift away into "semi-consciousness," he recommended that they introduce a desired idea into the minds, for example, "I will be relaxed tomorrow." Coué understood that this method allowed a bridge to be created between the conscious and unconscious mind, enabling the unconscious mind to bring about a desire – to make a wish come true.

Carl Jung, in the twentieth century, used a healing technique referred to as "active imagination." Jung instructed his patients to commence meditation without any program or goal in mind. Jung directed that any images that came to the patient's consciousness were to be observed and experienced without interference. At a later point in time, Jung would encourage the patient to communicate with the images by conversing with them and also by asking them questions. Active imagination was used to help the person appreciate their inner life and draw upon its healing power in seasons of stress. Gestalt and Jungian therapists have since then devised numerous stress reduction techniques using the imaginative and intuitive part of the mind.

Today, visualization is studied and practiced in pain and cancer centers throughout the country. Gawain states that visualization is a type of energy that creates life's happenings and life itself. Therefore, our mind creates our world, just as a movie projector projects images upon a blank screen.

SYMPTOM-RELIEF EFFECTIVENESS
Visualization is known to treat many physical and stress-related illnesses, including muscle spasms, headaches, chronic pain, and situation-specific or general anxiety. Visualization can be used to boost chemotherapy's effects, increase focus in sports competition, prepare patients for surgery, and to enhance well-being.

TIME TO MASTER
Symptom relief can be instantaneous or may take several weeks to master.

INSTRUCTIONS

Types of Visualization

Everybody visualizes. Memories, daydreams, and inner talk are types of visualization. You can harness your visualizations and employ them to improve your life.

Visualization

Visualizations are mental sense impressions that you create consciously to relieve stress and relax your body.

There are three main types of visualization:

1. Receptive visualization:

   With this type, you empty your mind, relax, sketch a scenery, ask a question, and await a response. For example, imagine that you are on a beach and that the sea breeze is gently caressing your skin. You can smell and hear the sea. You might ask, "Why am I not able to relax?" and the answer might surface into your consciousness, e.g., "Because you cannot say no to people," or "Because you cannot detach yourself from your friends' depression."

2. Programmed visualization:

   Create an image, replete with sounds, sights, smells, and tastes. Imagine a goal that you desire to attain or healing that you wish to accelerate. For instance, Harriet utilized programmed visualization in her running. For her first race, Harriet visualized her race daily, on that particular course. She envisioned herself running up a hill, the pressure, heat and exertion, the exhaustion after several miles, and finally, the sprint to the finish line. Harriet eventually set a state record for her age group.

3. Guided visualization:

   Visualize your scene in detail. However, omit crucial elements. Wait for your subconscious, your inner guide, to provide the missing pieces of your puzzle. Jane imagines a special place, a forest clearing, that she traveled to as a Girl Scout, where she liked to relax. She constructs the sounds, smells, tastes, sights, and touch associated with the place. She imagines herself roasting marshmallows at twilight, over a warm campfire (there are no mosquitoes).

She imagines someone she loves, her Girl Scout leader, and Jane asks the leader for tips on how to relax. Sometimes the Scout leader reminds Jane of songs she loved to sing, and she encourages Jane to sing them when she feels tense. Other times she reminds Jane of campfire games, old jokes, and old times that Jane enjoyed, and which made her laugh; she instructs Jane to laugh more.

The leader gives Jane a warm hug and reminds her that she is loved, that she needs to look for affirmations of that love.

Rules for Effective Visualization

1. Get a quiet place. Loosen any tight clothing, lie down, and close your eyes
2. Scan your body, seek tension in specific muscle groups. Relax those muscles as much as is possible
3. Form mental sense impressions. Involve your senses: hearing, taste, sight, touch, and smell. For instance, imagine that you are in the middle of a beautiful green forest, gazing at a vivid blue sky with fluffy white clouds. Add sounds to the vision: water running, wind in the trees, birdcalls, pine needles crunching underfoot, and so on. Imagine the ground under your feet, the smell of pine, mountain spring water, or the taste of a stem of grass.
4. Use affirmations. Repeat simple, positive statements that affirm your new ability to relax. Use present tense and avoid negatives, e.g., "I am not tense," in favor of "I am letting go of tension."

   Examples of affirmations are:
   I am in harmony with life.
   I can relax at will.
   Peace is within me.
   Tension flows from my body

5. Practice visualization three times a day. Practice is easiest when done first thing in the morning and at night when lying in bed. After training, visualization will be possible at the service station, before a parent-teacher conference and even when waiting in the doctors' office – even during an IRS audit.

BASIC TENSION AND RELAXATION EXERCISES

1. Eye Relaxation (Palming)

   Close your eyes. Place your palms lightly over your eyelids. Without putting too much pressure, block out all light. Try to see the color black. While you may see other images or colors, focus on the color black. Use a mental image to visualize the color black (a black object in the room, black fur). Continue this way for one to three minutes, as you think, and focus on the color black. Lower your hands and open your eyes. Gradually adjust to the light. Experience the relaxation in the muscles surrounding your eyes

2. Metaphorical Images

   Lie down and close your eyes. Relax. Visualize an image that causes tension and replace it with an image that causes relaxation. The best images are those that you make up yourself. To get started, some suggestions include the following:

   The color red
   The confinement of a dreary tunnel
   The glare of a searchlight
   The pounding of a jackhammer
   The scream of a police siren in the night
   The screech of white chalk on a blackboard
   The smell of ammonia
   The tension of a cable

   These tension images during the process of visualization can expand, soften, and fade, creating harmony and relaxation:
   The cable can slacken
   The chalk can crumble into fine powder
   The color red can fade and become pale blue
   The dreary tunnel can open into an airy and sunlit beach
   The jackhammer can transform into the hands of an expert masseuse kneading your muscles
   The searchlight might fade and become a soft rosy glow
   The police siren can soften into the whisper of a flute
   The smell of ammonia can become the scent of lemon or a rose

As you scan your body, start by applying a tension image to a tense muscle and then let it develop into a relaxation image. For example, with a stiff neck, visualize a tightened vise. To relax, imagine the vise opening when you say the affirmation "I can relax at will" or "Relax." End by reciting your affirmation. Speak to the tenseness as you use your relaxation image. Monitor what happens to your tension.

3. Creating Your Special Place

   When creating a special place, your intention should be to make a refuge for guidance and relaxation. This place can be located either indoors or outdoors. Follow the following guidelines when structuring your place:

   - Include a private entry into your special place
   - Make room for an internal guide or any other person to be in that room with you comfortably
   - Design your place and fill it with enticing detail. Create a foreground, middle ground, and background
   - Make it comfortable, peaceful, and safe

   Example 1:

   A special place can be at the end of a winding path that leads to a glistening pond. Green grass is as a carpet under your feet, mountains are in the distance and the pond is twenty yards away. The air is cool against your skin in this shady spot. The sun is bright, and a mockingbird is singing. The honeysuckle's pungent odor attracts bees, which buzz over the flowers, drawn to their sweet nectar.

   Example 2:

   Your special place can be a sparkling clean kitchen, with Cinnabon's baking in the oven. You can see fields of wheat through the kitchen window. A chime flutters in the gentle breeze. You've prepared a cup of herbal tea for your guest. Record this exercise and play it, or get a friend to read it aloud.

   Now, let's visualize:

   Lie down, go to your safe place, and be totally comfortable. Close your eyes and mentally walk to a quiet place. That place can be located either inside or outside. It should be safe and peaceful.

Notice the view in the distance. Picture yourself unloading your anxieties and worries. What do you hear? What do you smell? What is in front of you? How does it feel? Hear it, smell it, reach out, and touch it. Adjust the temperature so that you can be comfortable. Feel safe in that special place.

Look around for a private spot, an exceptional spot. Feel the ground under your feet and find the path to the special spot. Look above you, what do you see? What do you hear and smell? Walk on this path until you enter your quiet, comfortable, safe spot. You have now arrived at your special place, in a private spot.

What is under your feet? Take several steps. How does it feel? What do you hear? What do you see above you? Reach out and touch something. What does it feel like? What is its texture? Are there any pens, paints, paper nearby, or is there a sandy shore to draw in, or clay to work? If there are, go to them, smell them, handle them.

These are your special tools that your inner guide can use to reveal feelings and ideas to you. Gaze into the distance, as far as your eyes can see. What can you see? What aromas do you notice? Lie or sit in your special place. Nothing can harm you in your special place. Notice and memorize its sounds, smells, and sights. If you sense any danger, expel it. Realize that you are comfortable, safe and relaxed. Spend two to five minutes to realize that you are relaxed. Return to this place to relax whenever you please. Leave by the same path and entrance. As you do so, notice the ground and touch things near you. Look into the distance and appreciate the view. Recite this affirmation "This is my special place and I can visit whenever I wish" or "I can relax here."

Now open your eyes and appreciate your relaxation.

4. Finding Your Inner Guide

Your inner person should be a construct of a calmer you, or an imaginary person who instructs or clarifies. This construct is your connection to your subconscious and inner wisdom. Your inner person can clarify what is causing your stress. With a bit of practice, you can invite and connect with your inner wiser self whenever you want, in your special place. Try this exercise, record this exercise, and play it, or get a friend to read it aloud.

Now, let's visualize:

Follow the path to your spot. Relax, and invite your inner person to that special place. Watch your inner person approach, as a speck in the distance. Listen to the footsteps. Can you smell your wiser self's fragrance? If you feel unsafe in any way, send your inner person away. When you are comfortable, ask your inner self questions and wait for the answers. The answer can be a saying, a laugh, a feeling, a frown, or a dream. Ask your inner self, "What is causing my tension? How can I relax?" When your inner you responds, you may be surprised by the clarity and simplicity of the answers provided. Before you leave your special place, or when your inner you leaves that spot, say this affirmation to yourself, "I can relax at will" or "I can relax here."

Do this exercise for at least seven days, several times a day. On or before the seventh day, you'll probably have received some clarity and answers.

5. Listening to Music

Listening to music is one of the best and most common forms of relaxation. Each person will give special meaning to their choice in music. Some songs will remind them of happy times while others will remind them of sad times. It is, therefore, important to select music that is soothing and peaceful and suitable for relaxation.

If possible, buy or create an hour-long recording of uninterrupted and relaxing music. Play it daily or whenever you choose, in order to relax via music. Play any music that helped you relax in previous stressful seasons as it will likely benefit you in future stressful situations.

Make time to be alone, to get the most out of the music therapy session. Half an hour of uninterrupted quiet time should be sufficient. Put on the music that you have chosen, settle into a comfortable seat, and close your eyes. Mentally scan your body, note areas of pain, tension, and relaxation. Focus on the music while being aware of your mood. Each time an unrelated thought comes to mind, make a note of it, discard it, and remember your goal of music listening and relaxing.

Say an affirmation, such as "Music relaxes me" or "Relax." When the music ends, let your mind scan over your body again. Become aware of how you feel. Do you feel different? Any improvement to your attitude, mood, or well-being?

SPECIAL CONSIDERATIONS

1. Work on your most potent sense, if you have trouble perceiving impressions from the other senses. The other senses will improve in due time

2. Practice three times a day. Be patient. It takes time

3. If making a recording doesn't work, you may buy one

4. Remember to laugh. Laughter reduces physical and emotional tension because it produces internal massage. Hearty laughter stimulates your respiratory, circulatory, vascular, and nervous systems

5. As the spasms of laughter subside, the internal pressure that's released reduces muscle tension. That overall process creates a feeling of well-being

6. Laughter helps you remove your focus from your situation and yourself. Laughter helps you not take life too seriously and will improve your sense of well-being when practiced regularly

Autogenics

In this chapter on autogenics, you will learn to:

- Calm your mind
- Use verbal commands to relax
- Restore your body to a normal and balanced state
- Resolve specific physical problems

BACKGROUND

Autogenic training (AT) got its beginning from hypnosis research conducted by the famous physiologist Oskar Vogt. Vogt trained his most experienced hypnotic subjects to go into a self-trance that resulted in the reduction of their tension, fatigue, and painful symptoms, e.g., headaches. It also seemed to help the patients deal with their everyday lives more effectively. The subjects reported that when their tension and fatigue lifted, they felt heavy and warm.

A Berlin psychiatrist, Schultz, became interested in Vogt's work. He discovered that his patients could get into a state similar to a hypnotic trance by thinking of warmth and heaviness in their extremities. Essentially, all they needed to do was relax, sit comfortably, be undisturbed, and concentrate passively on verbal instructions that suggested that they feel heaviness and warmth in their limbs. Shultz combined Vogt's autosuggestions with yoga techniques to create the Autogenic Training system.

In its present form, Autogenic Training (AT) frees you from depending on a hypnotist. It also provides you with the healing effects of traditional hypnosis. With skillful use of AT, you can induce the feelings of heaviness and warmth associated with relaxation.

The four main categories of AT verbal formulas (exercises) are:
1. Verbal formulas to normalize the body
2. Verbal formulas to calm the mind
3. Meditative exercises to develop creativity and mental concentration
4. Autogenic exercises designed to address precise problems

This chapter on autogenics will teach you how to use verbal suggestions to calm your mind, help you resolve specific problems, and relax your mind. The verbal formulas used to normalize the body feature under six standard themes. The formulas are aimed at resolving and reversing the fight-or-flight instinct, or high-alarm state, which occurs when anyone experiences emotional or physical stress.

1. Heaviness is the first standard theme.
It promotes relaxation of the voluntary muscles, which are used to move your legs and arms. There are seven verbal formulas which suggest the theme of heaviness (AT verbal formulas, Set 1)

2. Warmth is the second theme.
Warmth brings about peripheral vasodilation. "My right hand is warm," is the verbal formula used to relax the blood vessels in your hand, so that, that warming blood can flow into your hand. This formula works to reverse the pooling of blood that collects in the head and trunk, during the fight-or-flight response to stress.

3. Normalizing cardiac activity is the focus of the third standard theme.
"My heartbeat is regular and calm" is the verbal formula.

4. Regulating the respiratory system is the focus of the fourth standard theme.

"It breathes me" is the verbal formula.

5.   Warming and relaxing the abdominal region is the focus of the fifth standard theme. "My solar plexus is well" is the verbal formula.

6.   The reduction of blood flow to the head is the focus of the sixth standard theme. "My forehead is cool" is the verbal formula.

The verbal formulas are used in conjunction with the six themes, and they serve to intensify the theme's effects.

SYMPTOM-RELIEF EFFECTIVENESS

Autogenic training (AT) is useful for treating muscle tension, the gastrointestinal tract (spasms, constipation, gastritis, diarrhea, and ulcers), disorders of the respiratory tract (bronchial asthma and hyperventilation), the circulatory system (irregular heartbeat, racing heart, high blood pressure, headaches, and cold extremities), and the endocrine system (thyroid problems). AT is also useful in the reduction of irritability, general anxiety, and fatigue. It can be employed to increase your resistance to stress, modify your reaction to pain, and eliminate or reduce sleeping disorders.

CONTRAINDICATIONS

AT is not recommended for children under five years of age, or people who lack motivation, or those with severe emotional or mental disorders. Before beginning AT, you must have a physical exam and discuss with your medical doctor about the physiological effects of AT. Those with serious diseases, for example, diabetes, heart conditions, or hypoglycemic conditions, should be under a medical doctor's supervision while undergoing autogenics training.

Some people may experience increased blood pressure, while a few may have dramatically lowered blood pressure when they participate in AT exercises. If you have low or high blood pressure, you should monitor your blood pressure and check with your medical doctor to ascertain that AT is regularizing it. If you feel restless or very anxious during or after AT exercises, or have recurring disquieting side effects, discontinue AT and only resume exercising under the supervision of a certified AT instructor. Autogenic instructor training is offered at some universities and is practiced by mental health therapists, educators, and complementary medicine practitioners.

TIME TO MASTER

In the past, AT specialists advised moving slowly but surely at a steady pace, which would result in using up several months to master all six themes. This timetable is unrealistic because of people who typically get positive results in the first session of AT. Others require one to two weeks of constant practice to experience relaxation. Schedule your autogenic formulas for twice a day and twenty minutes per session. If you find that this is too much, shorten the length of each session and increase more sessions each day.

At the end of one solid month of practice, you may be able to relax by using all six themes. Thereafter, you may choose to utilize all six themes in a single twenty-minute relaxation exercise, or incorporate a few themes that bring about deep relaxation, rapidly. For instance, the formulas "My heartbeat feels calm and regular," and "My arms and legs feel warm and heavy," and "It breathes me" may induce immediate relaxation. Find out what theme works best for you by experimenting with a combination of themes.

INSTRUCTIONS

How to Facilitate Relaxation When Doing AT

- Choose a quiet room so that you won't be interrupted
- Keep the room at a moderately warm and comfortable temperature
- Minimize external stimuli
- Turn the lights down low
- Wear loose clothing

Select one of the following basic three AT postures:

1. Sit upright in an armchair, with your back, head, and extremities are supported. Make sure that you are comfortable
2. When seated on a stool, stoop over slightly, and rest your arms on your thighs, with your neck relaxed, and your hands draped lightly between your knees

3. With your head supported, lie on your back, with your legs eight inches apart, toes pointed slightly outward and arms resting at your sides, comfortably, without touching your body

- Scan your body to ensure that your preferred position is tension-free. Watch out for overextension of your limbs, e.g., unsupported arms or head, a crooked spine, legs, or tightening of the limbs at joints. If you observe any of these overextensions, continue moving and adjusting your position until you are well-supported, comfortable and without any overextensions
- Pick a point to focus on or close your eyes softly
- Take a few deep and very slow, relaxing breaths before you start reciting your autogenic formulas.

Practice How to Normalize Your Body with the Six Basic

Autogenic Themes

There are two main ways in which to learn the six autogenic themes.

The first is to create a recording of all the verbal formulas and listen to it once or twice a day. Alternatively, memorize and practice one set of formulas, until you include all the themes into your practice. Slowly repeat each formula to yourself, keeping up a steady and silent verbal stream.

As a general rule, slowly repeat each formula four times. Say it slowly (five seconds) and then pause for about three seconds.

For example, if you use the first three formulas of the first set, you'd say to yourself:
- "My right arm is heavy" (four times repeatedly). This should take about half a minute
- You could also say to yourself, "My left arm is heavy" (four times repeatedly)
- And, "Both of my arms are heavy" (four times repeatedly)

The entire set should take less than four minutes. If you are intent on memorizing one set, repeat the set up to 20 minutes in one practice session. You can also create several mini-practice sessions from one or a few more sets daily. If recording the formulas, leave about half a minute in between individual verbal formulas for silent repetition.

As you quietly repeat a verbal formula, be careful to "passively concentrate" on the section of the body it refers to. In other words, notice what happens without any judgments or expectations. Passive concentration does not mean going to sleep or spacing out. Remain alert to the experience while not analyzing it. This casual attitude is later on contrasted with active concentration, which occurs when you focus your attention on specific aspects of your experience. You should have a goal-directed investment and interest in it. Active concentration is essential, just as is the case when fixing a car or preparing a new recipe. Passive concentration is a necessary requirement for relaxation.

Initially, you won't be able to maintain passive concentration successfully. Expect your mind to wander. That is natural. Immediately return to the formula when you find that you are losing focus. In addition, you may also experience symptoms referred to as "autogenic discharges" that are normal but distracting. Some examples are, you may sense stiffness, a change in your weight or temperature, anxiety, illusions, tingling, involuntary movements, "electrical currents," some pain, a desire to cry, headaches, irritability, or nausea.

Other times, you may experience feelings of bliss or fascinating insights. Whether you have unpleasant or pleasant experiences, note them and then return to your AT formulas. Remember that all these experiences are transitory and aren't the purpose of AT. They will pass as you proceed with the practice.

When you are ready to end an AT session, say, "When I open my eyes, I will feel alert and refreshed." Open your eyes, take in a few deep breaths, stretch and flex your arms. Be sure that you aren't still in a trancelike state when you resume your regular activities.

Please note: Before you begin practicing AT, read the cautionary notes and helpful hints at the end of this chapter, in the Special Considerations section.

Set 1

Both of my arms are heavy
Both of my legs are heavy
My arms and legs are heavy
My left arm is heavy
My left leg is heavy
My right arm is heavy

My right leg is heavy

Set 2

Both of my arms are warm

Both of my legs are warm

My arms and legs are warm

My left arm is warm

My right arm is warm

My right leg is warm

Set 3

Both of my arms feel heavy and warm

Both of my legs feel heavy and warm

It breathes me

My legs and arms feel heavy and warm

My heartbeat is calm and regular

My right arm is heavy and warm

Set 4

It breathes me

My limbs feel heavy and warm

My heartbeat is calm and regular

My right arm is heavy and warm

My solar plexus is warm

Set 5

It breathes me

My legs and arms feel heavy and warm

My forehead is cool

My heartbeat is calm and regular

My right arm is heavy and warm

My solar plexus is warm

Autogenic Formulas for Calming the Mind

The following formulas focus less on physical functions and more on mental tasks. They reinforce the autogenic verbal formulas for the previously mentioned six standard themes.

Here's a list of examples:

You may add any combination of these mind-calming phrases at the end of every set of autogenic verbal formulas. However, for excellent results, be sure to intersperse them throughout each set.

For example, the first set can be rewritten as follows:

Both of my arms are heavy

Both of my legs are heavy

Deep within my mind, I visualize and experience myself as comfortable, relaxed and still

I am calm and relaxed

I am calm and relaxed

I am calm and relaxed

I am calm and relaxed

I am calm and relaxed

I am calm and relaxed

I am calm and relaxed

I feel an inward quietness

I feel quite quiet

I withdraw my thoughts from my current surroundings. I feel serene and still

My left arm is heavy

My left leg is heavy

My mind is quiet

My right arm is heavy

My right leg is heavy

My thoughts are turned inward. I am at ease

My whole body feels heavy, quiet, comfortable, and relaxed

Autogenic Modification Exercises

After you have mastered all six basic autogenic themes, practice autogenic modification by creating what Schultz referred to as "organ specific formulae" to resolve specific problems.

For example, you may develop a formula (indirect) such as "My shoulders are warm" or "My feet are warm" each time you feel a warm and embarrassing blush coming on. Autogenic modification allows you to focus on something other than the blushing passively. You might also make use of a direct formula such as "My forehead is cool."

When you experience tension or persistent muscle pain in a part of your body, to become relaxed, use the autogenic verbal formulas. Also, passively concentrate on the painful or persistently tense area and project the feeling of warm and comfortable relaxation into that area. Repeat to yourself, "My [painful or tense or area] is comfortably relaxed and warm."

If you have frequent headaches, pay attention to the area that tightens up the most at the beginning of any headache. For instance, if it's your shoulders, neck, or back of the head aching, passively concentrate on that area. Project the sensation of relaxation into it while repeating to yourself, "My [mention area] is comfortable, warm, and relaxed." You may intersperse the verbal formula with "My forehead feels comfortable and cool."

Never suggest "My forehead feels warm" for the simple reason that those words would cause vasodilation, which would result in pain. When troubled by a cough, use the formula "My chest is warm. My throat is cool." With asthma, add to the usual formula "It breathes me, it breathes me calm and regular."

You are highly suggestible toward the end of an AT session. Because you are in a highly relaxed state, it is a good time as any to use the "intentional formulae." With this method, you tell yourself how to do difficult tasks. For example, to quit smoking, you can repeatedly, "Smoking is a dirty habit. I can live without it." If you want to eat less, say, "I have control over what I eat. I can eat less and be more attractive." These intentional formulas should be persuasive, believable, and brief.

SPECIAL CONSIDERATIONS

1. Start with your dominant arm, when practicing the six themes: begin with your left arm, if you write with it. Say, "My right arm is heavy" (repeat four times), and then move to the phrase, "My right arm is heavy" (repeat four times), and so on.

2. If you are unable to experience the physiological sensations suggested by verbal formulas, give imagery a try. Contemplate being in a warm shower or luxurious bubble bath, or having your hand comfortably submerged in a warm basin of water. Imagine yourself sitting in the sun or drinking a delicious mug of your favorite hot chocolate. Think about warm blood flowing through your body, fingertips, and toes. Imagine lying on a comfortable and heavy warm blanket or lying at the beach under heavy sand. Recall the sensation of a cool breeze or cool washcloth against your forehead.

3. Note that about 10 percent of people experimenting with AT never experience sensations of warmth or heaviness. This doesn't matter. The formulas describing heaviness and warmth are generally used to bring about functional change in the body, that you may or may not feel. Focus on doing the formulas correctly, and you should experience sensations of relaxation, within two weeks of practice

4. Some people may experience a paradoxical response when they begin practicing autogenic verbal formulas. For example, they might feel light even as they recite the verbal formulas for heaviness. They might feel cool as they repeat the formulas for warmth. Don't worry. The body is reacting to the formulas and will relax in due time

5. If you experience unpleasant side effects with one theme, move to a next one and return to the difficult formula at the end of the training

6. If you find it difficult to become aware of your heartbeat, lie on your back and rest your hand over your heart. Should you experience distress or discomfort, move on to another theme and later on return to this one, or skip it

7. In the instance that you have diabetes, ulcers, or any condition involving internal bleeding in abdominal organs, don't say, "My solar plexus is warm." Lie down if you notice lightheadedness or dizziness when saying, "My forehead is cool."

Work-Stress Management

In this chapter, you'll learn how to:

- Counter stressful thoughts about work
- Identify how you respond to stress in a work environment
- Negotiate when in conflict
- Pace and balance yourself
- Take control of work-related stress

BACKGROUND

Classic symptoms of work burnout are increased dissatisfaction, absenteeism, pessimism, and inefficiency at the job. Though you may not be suffering from work burnout, your work situation may be a constant source of stress. Job stress accounts for personal misery and billions of dollars lost annually in wages, productivity, and medical bills. Americans have realized that managing work-related stress makes personal and financial stress.

WHAT CAUSES WORK BURNOUT?

Every job includes difficulties that a worker is compensated to adjust to. Job difficulty on its own does not cause burnout – it can also be the workers' inability to control his/her work situation, which leads to frustration, uncertainty, reduced motivation, reduced productivity, fatigue, and eventually burnout.

Other factors that can lead to burnout:
- Chronic work overload
- Impossible expectations of your boss
- Inadequate training
- Lack of clear direction about priorities
- Lack of recognition or rewards
- Unfair treatment
- Unpleasant work environment
- Unsupportive or hostile coworkers
- Personal values that are in conflict with the boss, coworkers, and or company

Even simple factors that are beyond your control can cause stress. Consider the numerous interruptions that occur during your workday: e-mail, special meetings, people dropping in, phone calls, and equipment breakdowns. Think about all the bureaucratic red tape when navigating authorization channels. Think about faulty air-conditioning systems, elevator music, the constant din of machines, and chattering voices around the water cooler. Your daily commute may also add to your accumulated stress.

It is erroneous to associate excessive stress with reduced productivity. The phenomenon of stress underload occurs when a task is too easy or insufficiently challenging. The symptoms of stress underload are similar to stress overload: irritability, a sense of time pressure, poor judgment, reduced efficiency, diminished motivation, and accidents. Every human being has a unique "performance zone," where an individual is able to experience manageable stress that stimulates our motivation, decision making, energy, and productivity.

To resolve burnout through stress management, find the right types and amounts of a challenge to stimulate your performance and interest without overloading you. A tedious job environment is also stressful. Finally, balance leisure and work-related activities – balance is key.

SYMPTOM-RELIEF EFFECTIVENESS
Work-stress management increases your sense of personal control in the workplace. Feelings of personal power can improve work-related symptoms of anxiety, depression, guilt, and low self-esteem. Work-place stress management can reduce work-related psychosomatic symptoms such as fatigue, eating disorders, insomnia, headaches, upset stomach, and lowered immunity to infection.

TIME TO MASTER
Over the next couple of days, be keen to observe how you currently respond to work stressors, and set a few goals for change. Be patient as it will take at least one month to respond effectively to job stress and two-six months to fully integrate new work habits into your daily life.

FIVE STEPS TO MANAGE WORK STRESS
Step 1: Identify How You Respond to Stress at Work
What stresses you at work, and how do you respond to it? Observe your response to both big and small work stressors for a few days. Reflect on recent experiences at work and identify any adverse reactions you may have had.

In the following form, list your specific stresses in the My Response To Work Stressors. For each stressful item, jot down your feelings on the day the stress occurred, what you said to yourself about it, and what you did in response to it.

For example, Roda, a computer programmer, wrote about specific stressors in her job in the following manner:

MY RESPONSE TO WORK STRESSORS			
Your Work Stressor	Your Feelings	Your Thoughts	Your Behavior
Programming	Bored, numb	"Nonstop programming makes Roda a dull girl."	Inefficient, plodding; Drink coffee, eat sweets
Deadlines	Anxious	"I'll never make it!"	Work longer and faster, have errors
Meetings	Annoyed, impatient	"What a waste; I've got work to do."	Critical, resistant to suggestions
Vague supervisor	Insecure, annoyed, confused	"What will it take to please this human being?"	Guess what he wants, complain

Exercise: Using the above example, list your specific stressors below and describe your response. Use as much detail as you need.

MY RESPONSE TO WORK STRESSORS

Your Work Stressor	Your Feelings	Your Thoughts	Your Behavior

Exercise: Now write down troublesome patterns to your response to stress. For example, Roda wrote:

My Problematic Responses to Work Stress
1. I overeat and drink excessive amounts of coffee in response to the boredom I feel at work
2. Working for long periods at a busy computer terminal causes me a myriad of emotional and physical symptoms of stress
3. I waste time due to my inability to say no to workmates, ask my supervisor questions, or request administrative support

Write the patterns in the blank My Problematic Responses to Work Stress form below.

My Problematic Responses to Work Stress
1.
2.
3.
4.
5.
6.
7.
8.

9.
10.

Step 2: Set Goals to Respond Effectively to Work Stress

Now that you have identified patterns of stress in your workplace, formulate an effective plan to respond to those stressors. Perhaps you can avoid a few of those stressors altogether. Maybe you can be more prepared to face them when they happen. Taking control and exercising your power is the name of the game, and you can do so now.

You'll probably want to change one or more of the following areas:

1. Change the external stressor (assertively request your boss, not to overload you, quit the job, reorganize your time, take regular breaks)

2. Change your thoughts (stop dwelling on old injustices and vague worries, turn off work when you get home, don't assume that you are responsible for other peoples problems, drop your perfectionist attitude)

3. Change physically (exercise, relax, get sufficient sleep, eat properly)

When drawing up goals for yourself, remember that attainable goals are:

a) Specific

b) Observable

c) Achievable within a certain time frame

d) Broken down into small intermediate steps

e) Compatible with long-term goals

f) Written down in the self-contract form

g) Reevaluated at specified intervals

h) Rewarded when achieved

For example, Roda decided to set new and effective responses to the four stress patterns. To that end, Roda wrote the following self-contract:

Exercise: Write out your goals using the Self-Contract form below

January 2020

I, Roda, agree to change four old patterns pertaining to my response to stress in the following ways:

Patterns 1 and 2: Instead of drinking coffee or eating junk when I am bored, tired, or frustrated, I'll get up, walk around and talk to people; I will take regular breaks every hour and do a brief relaxation exercise; I'll take advantage of flextime and go to an aerobics class at least three days a week; I'll run personal errands twice a week during lunch break; Instead of snacking on junk food, I'll eat three nutritious meals a day

Pattern 3: I'll enroll in an assertiveness training workshop and will ask my supervisor questions to clarify what he needs me to do, until I comprehend his instructions. I'll also tell my chatty coworker not to distract or interrupt me; I'll be available to chat during lunch break only. I will assertively and boldly ask the admin assistant for help.

Pattern 4: I will take each critical thought and convert it into a constructive thought. For instance, when I think about meetings, "What a waste of time, I have so much work to do," I will say and think, "Wonderful, a break from programming! I may learn something new and exciting. I could do some discreet relaxation exercises. Also, I may contribute something to the meeting.

I will check my progress weekly and reevaluate accordingly.

After one month of progress, I will reward myself with a weekend at a spa. Over the next couple of months, I hope to improve my levels of satisfaction in the workplace.

Roda Sky

Post this contract, where you will see it every day so that it may serve as a reminder of what you are to do. You may also share the contract with a coworker or friend who can support and encourage you to follow through with your plan. Report back to that person on a weekly basis by providing a report on your progress toward each goal. Reward yourself each time you achieve your objectives.

Use the blank Self-Control form below:

Date:

I, _____, agree to:

1.
2.
3.
4.
5.
6.

I will monitor my progress every _____ (length of time).

I will reward myself with _____.

Name: _____

Signature: _____

Step 3: Change Your Thinking

Work stress occurs because your thoughts trigger painful emotions. Here a three negative thoughts that'll worsen your situation:

1. I've got to do _____(a particular task)_____ (on time) (perfectly) (so that my boss will be pleased) or _____ (something painful) will happen

2. They are doing this to me and it is not fair

3. I am trapped here

The first thought causes you anxiety, the second makes you angry, and the third generates depression. You can change these thoughts and the stress that they create.

List the things that you tell yourself about your work environment, which fit into the above three categories.

Category 1:

_____

_____

_____

_____

Category 2:

_____

_____

_____

_____

Category 3:

_____

_____

_____

_____

Here is how you can manage these stress-producing thoughts:

1. Realistically consider the possibilities of what would happen if the task is not finished on time, totally pleasing to your boss, or absolutely flawless. A realistic appraisal means reflecting on the repercussions of submitting work late, with errors, and so on. Being realistic means being very specific in order to get rid of any vague sense of doom. Consider what your boss is likely to say. Think about what would happen; worst case scenarios.

    Example: "If I don't complete this report by Friday, my supervisor will likely tell me to work over the weekend to get the report done for Tuesday's meeting with the client. I'll have to postpone the luncheon and shopping with my friends. That's disappointing, but I can handle it."

    Exercise: Your turn. Rewrite each vague and catastrophic thought by filling in the blanks:
    "If _____ isn't _____ (perfect), (totally acceptable, on time), _____ is likely to happen (something realistic). I can handle it."

    Mentally recite this coping statement every time you have catastrophic thoughts. Note: If you do not know what will happen, find out your alternatives. For example, you can say, "Boss, if I'm two days late with the Ball report, will you be inconvenienced?"

2. Nothing good can be gained by blaming others for your work stress. Blaming ties you to a victim mentality, and maintains your sense of feeling trapped, helpless, and stuck. Blaming encourages you to think that you don't have any alternatives and that you have lost the power of choice. Blaming triggers stress and anger hormones, e.g., adrenaline, which depletes your energy and damages your health.

    Only you can take care of "you" and protect you at your workplace. Your supervisor and coworkers are busy protecting themselves. This is natural and an inescapable fact of life.

    Exercise: So how can we stop wasting any more energy on anger and blaming? Ask yourself, "What can I do to change my current circumstance and condition?"

    a) _____
       _____

b) _____

_____

c) _____

_____

If you cannot think of any ways in which to change your working conditions, you have two choices – you can either accept and adapt to current conditions or change your job.

Exercise: If you accept your current circumstances in your workplace, fill in the blanks:

_____ is acting exactly as she/he should. The conditions necessary for her/him to act this way (her/his needs and the coping strategies to meet those past successes and failures, needs, fears, and attitudes toward our relationship) exist, and this is why he/she did _____ (with)(to) me."

3. You are not trapped; what you are is a person with difficult choices – not trapped. You have the option to change your circumstances or do nothing.

Exercise: What steps could you take to transform a major stress producer at your job?

What steps can you take to change jobs?
What steps can you take to overcome the fear of change and perception of a risk to be able to attempt making a change?
What would you give up or risk in attempting that change?

Typically, this would involve you getting information to enable you to make an objective decision, while also giving you the confidence that you can cope with any potential challenges that could arise from making a change. For example, if you think that it is risky to change job at your age, look for someone your age who is employed in the position that you are interested in. Perhaps they can advise you on whether age is an important factor. Or, if you fear messing up a job interview, you can hire the services of a coach to help perfect your interview skills.

However, if you are not ready to take the risk to effect change, instead of claiming that you are trapped or stuck, say to yourself, "I choose to endure the current work situation because it seems less painful than putting in the effort to move. I may rethink my position in the near future."

Step 4: Negotiate When in Conflict

Whether your disagreement is with your supervisor regarding a salary increase, or with coworkers about brewing coffee, negotiate a compromise by assertively presenting your position.

Use the following four-step model when you want to discuss a problem with your coworkers or supervisor:

State:
1. The problem (what you think is the cause of your stress)
2. Your feelings about the problem
3. How the issue affects your motivation and productivity
4. A win-win solution (when both sides of the conflict gains from your solution)

Exercise: Negotiate a Mutually Acceptable Outcome

Think of something that you want at work which would require you to negotiate with someone. Fill in the following blanks:

The problem as I see it is: _____ I feel

_____ about this problem. It affects my motivation or productivity or

motivation in that _____ I suggest we try this win-win solution:

_____

Change the wording to fit your situation. Memorize this script, and then, look for a moment to share it with the individual whose cooperation you are seeking. Be open to hearing all interested parties' points of view. Look for a workable compromise that will benefit the two of you.

Step 5: Pace and Balance Yourself

When at work, do you pace yourself? Most jobs are like marathons and therefore require workers to pace themselves in order to cross the finish line without collapsing. Like a marathon runner, you'll need to conserve your energy to deal with anticipated items down the road, as well as surprises.

Eight tips for balancing and pacing yourself:

1. Pay attention to your natural work habits and natural rhythms in order to determine when you perform optimally. Schedule your most complicated tasks for that time of the day

2. Set up your day in a manner that will allow you to shift back and forth between simple, pleasant, and difficult tasks. After completing a tough assignment, schedule something enjoyable

3. Schedule work-related tasks that are enjoyable, albeit not productive. Try to observe this habit even on busy days when you feel rushed. These time periods must be sacrosanct

4. Take advantage of your lunches and coffee breaks to do things that will reverse the stress response. For example, withdraw to a quiet place and do e.g., yoga or a relaxation exercise. A fifteen-minute brisk walk will provide you with as much energy as a mug of coffee. An uplifting and humorous conversation with coworkers will release tension and help you get a fresh perspective on a work problem that is weighing you down

5. If you have a flexible schedule, take a long break and do some cardio or aerobic exercises, run personal errands, or a relaxation exercise

6. Take minibreaks throughout your day. This will prevent or reduce symptoms of stress and tension. These breaks should be a few minutes in duration, and the payoff will be seen in increased productivity and mental alertness

7. Choose leisure activities that balance out the unique pressures and stresses of your job. For example:

If your job requires:	Consider a complementary leisure activity such as:
Much sitting or mental	Aerobic exercise concentration

Mindless repetition	Intellectually challenging hobbies and interests
A controlled environment	Hiking in nature; adventure
Boring tasks or no	Competitive or achievement recognition -oriented activities
Responding to people's demands	Solitary activities
Dealing with conflicts	Peaceful activities
Working alone	Social activities

8. Plan carefully, the type and timing of vacation you go on, to maximize their recuperative efforts.

Exercise: List three ways that you pace yourself at work to create balance in your life:

1. _____

_____

2. _____

_____

3. _____

_____

FINAL THOUGHTS

Every so often, stress at work is to be expected. You will sometimes feel stressed by certain aspects of your job. This chapter has shown you that you have the power to reduce, even eliminate stress from your work environment. You have the ability to enact changes to help you decrease work stress.

Exercise and Anxiety Relief

Research shows that regular exercise is as effective as antidepressant medication, if not better, due to exercise not having any side effects. Exercise is also known to prevent anxiety; it increases our resistance to stress.

Try to get some form of physical activity at least three times a week. For the best results, combine 20 minutes of vigorous cardiovascular exercise with some weight training. As always, please consult a medical practitioner before taking up a rigorous work-out regimen.

HOW DOES EXERCISE REDUCE STRESS?

Exercise restores your body to its normal equilibrium. It accomplishes this by releasing natural chemicals that build up during the stress response. Exercise improves your resilience to stress in several ways. Some of the benefits of exercise are listed below.

Exercise produces the following results:

- It creates a sense of well-being while releasing endorphins into your bloodstream. This is sometimes referred to as the body's "natural high"
- Produces a relaxation response in one's body and mind by decreasing muscle tension caused by emotional stress
- It clears the mind by increasing alpha-wave activity in the brain. This enables you to concentrate and focus more easily
- Eliminates toxins in the body
- Improves posture and overall flexibility, thereby decreasing pain or spinal stiffness caused by stress
- Relieves chronic constipation and indigestion caused by stress
- Improves overall energy levels by lessening fatigue
- Produces more restful sleep by combating insomnia caused by stress
- Enables you to cope with the daily stresses of a modern and busy schedule and provides a natural outlet for daily pressures
- Strengthens your lungs and heart, improving health and the overall level of physical fitness

- Increases one's energy expenditure or resting metabolism, therefore, helping you to lose weight. With weight loss, you can shed stress-induced negative self-image because you look good and feel good
- Helps you appreciate your resolve and strength; if you can change your behavior and attitude toward exercise, you can manage any stress that's present in your life
- Nourishes the brain via improved blood flow to it, which also provides higher levels of oxygen and the elimination of waste products
- For those that have stress-related medical conditions, <u>exercise reduces health risks</u>. "The evidence is more convincing than ever, and steadily growing! People of all ages, and from all walks of life, who are physically inactive, can improve their stress levels, well-being, and overall health by becoming moderately active on a regular basis."

This last statement alone should be sufficient to motivate you to prioritize exercise as a primary method to reduce any stress in your life.

SAMPLE EXERCISE PROGRAM

Warm-Up for Exercise

Always prepare your body for exercise with gentle warm-up stretches so as to avoid putting sudden stress on your muscle groups. Warm-up exercises increase your body temperature and metabolism by increasing oxygen and blood flow to your lungs, heart, and muscles. Warm-up exercises prepare your body for vigorous exercise while lessening the chance of cramping, injury, and overall muscle soreness.

- Duration: Fifteen minutes of stretching and light aerobic activity before you begin your workout

Follow Warm-Up with Aerobics

The most readily available form of aerobic exercise is jogging and brisk walking. Therefore, a jogging and walking program is referred to in this section to demonstrate the principles of aerobic exercise. You can use a similar approach for cycling, running, swimming, jumping rope, cross-country skiing or any other aerobic activity you may choose to do.

Your large skeletal muscles tense and relax, stimulating blood flow through your veins, arteries, lungs, and heart. Your heart rate is critical because just as a car's speedometer tells you the speed, your heart rate reveals how hard you are working. Therefore, if you travel way too fast in your car, the speedometer indicates the high speeds, and you slow down; likewise, if driving too slowly, you speed up.

Whereas the speed of a car is measured in miles per hour, your heart rate is measured in beats per minute. You can establish your heart rate by taking your pulse. Practice by taking your pulse when sitting quietly. Wear a watch with digital seconds or a sweep second hand on your left arm.

A normal resting pulse can range from 40-100 beats per minute, depending on your physical fitness level. To benefit from aerobic exercise, a person's heart must reach a range called the "target heart rate" and stay there for at least 20 minutes. In this range, your heart is supposed to beat at a rate of between 60-75 percent of its maximum speed. Exercising at this pace stimulates relaxation, and it's the safest pace or exercise range for you.

Exercising places moderate stress on your heart, which is positive stress that improves heart efficiency by gradually strengthening the heart muscle. To be within safe exercising limits, be careful to monitor your heart rate during exercise, and compare it to your target rate. This good practice will give you immediate feedback about the level of intensity of the activity. If you are doing too much exercise, reduce the intensity and vice versa, if you are not doing enough, increase the intensity of the exercise routine.

If you find that your heart rate is more than the required target heart rate, slow down. However, if your heart rate when exercising is less, speed up. For out of shape exercisers, brisk walking may elevate your pulse to over 60 percent of the recommended target heart rate for your age group. As your body acclimatizes to exercising, and your lungs and heart become better conditioned, you will have to exert more effort by either walking or jogging faster to attain your target heart rate.

The following are three simple tests to determine how fast you must jog or walk in order to reach your target heart rate.

Test Number 1:

- Walk at a comfortable pace for a duration of five minutes
- Take your pulse immediately since the rate decreases immediately
- If your pulse is less than your age groups target heart rate, go to the second test
- If you have reached your target rate, walk at this pace daily, until your target heart rate drops below 60 percent of the maximum heart rate. When it does, go to the second test

Test Number 2:

- Walk at a vigorous pace for a duration of five minutes
- Take your pulse immediately since the rate decreases immediately
- If your pulse is less than your age groups target heart rate, go to the third test
- If you have reached your target rate, walk at this pace daily, until your target heart rate drops below 60 percent of the maximum heart rate. When it does, go to the third test

Test Number 3:

- Do one minute of slow jogging and one minute of brisk walking, alternating between the two, for a duration of five minutes
- Take your pulse immediately since the rate decreases immediately
- If your pulse is less than your age group's target heart rate, continue with the slow jogging-brisk walking, alternating exercise every other day. When your pulse drops below the target heart rate, increase the time spent jogging and decrease your walking time

At this stage, you will need to focus on your pulse rate by checking it frequently until you find a challenging pace that will maintain your target heart rate for 20 minutes. After that, monitor your pulse once a week to ensure that you are reaching your target heart rate.

As you become conditioned to exercising, you'll find that you will need to increase the time spent jogging or upgrade to running, in order to reach and remain within your target heart rate. A good exercise hack is; jog until you feel winded. If you can sing, you are not exercising hard enough. When you reach the point of feeling winded and unable to sing, slow down to a brisk walk for one minute. Please note, when jogging, you should be able to maintain a conversation without becoming excessively out of breath. If you cannot talk, you are jogging too fast.

End by Cooling Down:

A period of cooling down helps your body to safely return to its pre-exercise state while slowing your heart rate and also decreasing your body temperature and metabolism. A cool-down period also prevents muscle soreness. When running or jogging, always end your session with at least ten minutes of slow walking and stretches.

Take long, exaggerated steps while stretching your arms and legs. Shake your hands and let your arms dangle loosely at your sides. The toning and stretching exercises you used as warm-up may also be used for cooling down.

- Duration: Ten minutes of light aerobics or stretching after your workout

SPECIAL CONSIDERATIONS

Here are suggestions to help you avoid injuries:

- Have a physical checkup. If you are obese, out of shape, older, on regular medication, or recovering from an operation or serious illness, it is critically important that you consult a doctor or a health care provider before starting a regular exercise program
- Strictly follow any precautions received from your doctor or health care provider
- Start slowly and gradually build up your exercising regimen. Progress at a steady pace
- Establish realistic goals, monitor your progress and adjust any goals accordingly
- Spread out your exercise regimen over a week, instead of exercising only on weekends
- Reach and maintain any exercise within your target heart rate. If feeling breathless, slow down – when exercising, you should be able to conduct a conversation
- Do warm-up exercises before aiming for your target heart rate, and cool down post-exercising
- Drink plenty of fluids to restore the liquids lost during vigorous exercise
- Do not exercise when ill. Your body requires sufficient rest to heal and recover its previous state of health
- Do not exercise after large meals because blood flow to large muscles is limited

- Do not use arm or ankle weights if you have knee or ankle problems, or low-back pain. Weights add stress to your joints and back
- Wear comfortable shoes designed for high impact, which support your feet and ankles. Replace your running shoes every six months or after every 400-600 miles
- Wear lightweight, comfortable, and loose-fitting layers of clothing. Be conscious of the environmental temperature, and be ready to shed or add clothing accordingly. Also, during the aerobic and warm-up phases, remove clothing as your body temperature decreases and add-on clothing when cooling down
- Use any exercising equipment that's recommended for safety reasons, e.g., helmets
- Listen to your body. You should not have any acute or sharp pain after exercising, only a bit of soreness, which will fade after a few exercise sessions
- Contact your doctor if you develop any of the following symptoms once you have begun an exercise program:
    - Your heart rate begins to skip beats and becomes irregular
    - Your heart rate needs more than fifteen minutes to slow down
    - You feel intense pressure, tightness, or pain in your neck, shoulders, chest, and arms
    - You feel dizzy or nauseous
    - After mild exertion, you feel extreme breathlessness
    - You feel exhausted hours after completing your exercise session
    - Whenever you exercise, you experience sharp or acute pain anywhere in your body

Sticking with It

Congratulations! By purposing to exercise regularly, you have taken an important step toward reducing stress in your life. There are two major obstacles you will encounter when you start an exercise program. Getting started is the first. The second is keeping at it. Get started by following the instructions in the preceding sections. Choose exercise methods and physical activities that you enjoy. Select various types of exercises and cross-train to avoid boredom and to prevent your body from becoming used to any one kind of training activity. Stay with your exercise program so that it becomes routine. Finally, visualize success!

A Life Worth Living

If someone were to ask you, "What do you like to do to relax?" It is highly likely that you will say, for instance, "I watch TV," "I play golf," "I love to travel," or "I enjoy having dinner with friends." While these are not medically prescribed or scientific relaxation strategies, they are effective because they make us feel good about ourselves and others and/or they bring us pleasure. Activities that bring about happiness are the very things that anxiety tries to take away from us, therefore, making it vital for us to make time to do what brings about pleasure specifically.

For the purpose of discussion and exploration here, we outline two important causes of good feelings: mastery and pleasure. Mastery involves activities, such as sports or work, that require skill development; in constantly putting effort into a particular task, we can accomplish a lot while developing a sense of mastery. Pleasure involves activities that are embarked upon, for the sake of "play," and nothing else – for the simple reward of enjoying the activity. When pleasure and mastery are enjoyed in moderation, in conjunction with other activities, they can increase healthy emotions that promote the well-being of a person.

Pleasure and mastery activities, in addition to other skill-based activities, are used as distraction techniques. In the next section, we will list pleasure and mastery activities and show you how to alleviate anxiety with them.

Distraction Techniques

Pleasure Activities

Hobbies and other "play"

- Reading
- TV, movies, plays
- Dancing
- Playing or listening to music
- Board games or cards
- Arts and crafts, sewing, painting
- Cooking

- Walking, hiking, enjoying nature, fishing
- Sports (basketball, softball, swimming, etc.) or going as a spectator
- Martial arts (karate, etc.)
- Museums/zoos
- Video games
- Traveling, sightseeing, going to the beach, sunbathing
- Shopping
- Gardening/decorating
- Photography
- Comedy: TV, recordings, live
- Religion or spirituality

Social activities

- Spending time with family
- Enjoying own children and young relatives
- Enjoying close friends
- Hanging out with large groups of friends/acquaintances
- Parties, meeting new people
- Romance
- Pets
- Clubs: meeting people with similar interests
- Enjoying food and drink with others

List enjoyable activities in which you take part now or have enjoyed in the past. Add others from the list above that appeal to you or others that you think you might enjoy:

1. _____
2. _____
3. _____
4. _____
5. _____

Mastery Activities

Job or Meaningful Daytime Activity

Look for or attempt to develop some of these qualities in your occupation volunteer work, or other meaningful daytime activity:

• Enjoyment

• Creativity

• Feelings of competence (able to accomplish tasks satisfactorily)

• Potential for development of skills

• Ability to "move up" in the organization or take on more responsibility, if this is desired

• Social contact with coworkers, colleagues, others in the field

Other skill-based activities

• Sports

• Music practice and performance

• Home improvement/building

• Woodworking

• Visual art (painting, drawing, pottery, sewing, knitting

• Learning about interests (history, politics, food, language, culture, etc.)

List skill-based activities, such as work or sports, that are a part of your daily routine and lead to positive feelings and a sense of self-worth. Choose others from the list above or fantasize about possible activities that seem rewarding. Write them here.

1. _____

2. _____

3. _____

4. _____

5. _____

Diet and Mental Health

Eating a clean and balanced diet has been scientifically proven to improve energy levels, bring about, and maintain good health, as well as contribute to a good mood. Reduce and or totally eliminate junk food which is laden with chemicals and preservatives. Chemicals and preservatives in food have been shown to cause, or at the very least, exacerbate certain forms of mental illness.

There have been a number of food additives implicated in a number of mental issues. If you have any mental illness, try to stay away from the following additives.

- Aspartame (Equal, NutraSweet)

  This artificial sweetener is found in diet foods and sodas, and other low-calorie foods. There is evidence associating aspartame with several psychiatric disorders, including depression, panic attacks, and bipolar disorder. It is also known to aggravate memory problems.

- BHA and BHT

  Butylated hydroxytoluene (BHT) and butylated hydroxyanisole (BHA) are used to keep oils and fats from going rancid. BHT and BHA are found in chewing gum, cereals, potato chips, and vegetable oil to preserve freshness. Some people have reported in medical studies that their incidences of depression and anxiety subsided with the discontinuation of BHT and BHA.

- Food Coloring

  The United States permits artificial food colorings that certain studies claim aggravate ADHD symptoms. Research shows that disciplinary problems decreased, and academic performance increased, when artificial colors were eliminated from school food programs.

- Hydrogenated Vegetable Oil

  Trans fats are created in the process used to manufacture hydrogenated vegetable oil. Trans fats promote diabetes, heart disease, and depression.

- Monosodium glutamate (MSG)

  Studies report a link between neurodegeneration and excitotoxic damage that is caused by food additives such as MSG and artificial sweeteners. Excitotoxins cause sensitive neurons to die, and they have been linked to dementia and Alzheimer's disease.

- Sodium Nitrite (Sodium Nitrate)

  Sodium nitrite is used to preserve, color, and flavor ham, bacon, luncheon meats, hot dogs, smoked fish, corned beef and other cured and processed meat. Sodium nitrate has been linked to depression, memory loss, fatigue and anxiety.

Be aware of the source and quality of your food – try to eat organically sourced foods and food low in refined sugars. The quantity of food that you eat on a daily basis, that is, eating either too little or too much food, can affect your emotional health. For instance, people who consume a diet that is very low in carbohydrates have been shown to experience low energy levels and they often feel depressed and easily fatigued. On the flip side, those who binge on carbs may feel lethargic – moderation is key to a healthy mind, body and spirit.

Diet and Nutritional Therapy

Improper diet and poor nutrition can eventually result in the increase of blood acidity, accumulation of excess fat, and deterioration of the body's metabolism mechanism. This leads to headaches, fatigue, insomnia, mild depression, a lowered immune system, and anxiety. The symptoms are initially mild, but get more serious over a period of time.

Depression and anxiety may worsen even as health problems get severe. More severe health problems may also develop, for example, constipation, fatigue, digestive problems, skin problems, anemia, hormone imbalance, obesity, vague aches and pains, fatigue, high blood pressure, frequent infections, and even cancer. This type of progression is not part and parcel of the normal aging process.

For some people, nutritional deficiencies can be very serious and difficult to treat with only dietary adjustments. Some people might need high doses of minerals and vitamins. In situations of stress, nutritional supplements might be required. Nutritional therapy has evolved and is also used to treat symptoms of stress. Anyone suffering from stress needs to consume extra nutrients to reduce oxidative damage.

In addition to vitamin supplements, herbal medicine such as St. John's wort (Hypericum perforatum), ginkgo (Ginkgo biloba), kava (Piper methysticum), and valerian (Valeriana officinalis) are herbs commonly used in the treatment of mental health. In controlled clinical trials, all four herbs have been found to be as effective as pharmaceutical antidepressants.

Other Points to Consider

1. **Self-care**

   As seen in this comprehensive manual, coping with and overcoming anxiety requires a multifaceted strategy; we have to combine forces to prevent stress from interfering with our life goals. CBT provides the bulk of the necessary ammunition to wage war on anxiety, but other lifestyle factors are valuable as well. We discuss these factors below. Please consider them when assessing the strategies that you need to implement in combating anxiety. Give the following strategies a try and see if they help.

2. **Moderate and Balance Coping Skills**

   Address anxiety by using different approaches and angles – confront fear, problem solve, accept uncontrollable life circumstances, and modify your thinking when necessary. Take care of your mind and body while addressing the important elements of self-care that are listed below. Comprehend that "diversity" is the cardinal rule when it comes to coping with life's challenges and anxiety. The more coping methods and skills we develop in our life's journey, the more flexible and healthier we are, when difficulties arise.

3. **Treat Mental Illness**

   CBT skills are useful for managing anxiety. However, if an individual is presenting various forms of mental illness, they may need to get a thorough diagnosis and a treatment plan from a licensed psychologist/psychiatrist. If you are currently receiving therapy that is not working out, consider changing your therapist or at least the style of treatment. Consider "combination therapy," which combines an assortment of self-care, medication and therapy skills. Always consult a doctor and do not self-medicate.

4. **Confront Conflict**

   Learn how to confront conflicts, proactively, and diplomatically. Don't give room to a cyclical pattern of conflict or allow interpersonal conflicts to fester; learn how to be assertive and how to communicate in a manner that fosters peace. Perhaps being assertive is not an issue for you– in that case, you may simply need to learn how to relax and let things go!

5. **Treat Physical Illness**

Scientific research shows that there is a definite connection between one's mood, physical health and anxiety. Find out your family medical history, consult a doctor as needed, and be careful to take any prescribed medications.

6. **Sleep**

Numerous sleep studies show that the average adult needs an average of 8 hours of sleep every night. Insufficient sleep, or insomnia, is a known cause of anxiety. Therefore, getting at least 8 hours of uninterrupted sleep is important in the managing of anxiety and prevention of diseases such as high blood pressure, diabetes etc. Should you suffer from either sleep apnea or insomnia, please request a licensed therapist, or a mental health practitioner, to provide you with a referral letter for consultation with a sleep expert.

Avoid "mind-altering drugs," even those that are prescribed by a health practitioner. Prescriptions for mind-altering drugs should be a last recourse and not the first line of treatment. Therefore, only those diagnosed with chemical imbalances should receive prescriptions that introduce such drugs. For this reason, consult with licensed therapists who lean towards naturopathic treatment methods, rather than those that prescribe the most potent pharmaceutical drugs on the market for slightest mental illnesses with the – they cause more harm than good.

Entertainment and social drugs such as alcohol, nicotine, marijuana, caffeine, and other illicit drugs exacerbate anxiety. Discuss your use of any of these illicit drugs with your doctor; your mental health treatment plan might require that you stop consuming illegal drugs! Don't be afraid to disclose any long term addictions to your therapist – their intention is to help and not harm you.

7. **Social Support**

When we feel supported and accepted, we feel secure, safe, and happy. One approach in treating anxiety is to increase positive experiences by being around people who help us feel good about life and ourselves. The other way is to reduce symptoms.

8. **Slow Down**

   Ask yourself: "Am I overloaded with work so that I have to rush through everything to get it done? Do I ever get the chance to slow down, or do my days feel like one huge blur?" A fast-paced life communicates urgency to the brain. Whether those days constitute back-to-back work meetings, or planning leisure activities, in the long run, having dramatic days impacts our anxiety levels. This, in turn, raises blood pressure and causes one to become stressed. Do yourself a favor and cultivate a sense of calmness - pace yourself to reduce any sense of urgency.

9. **Time Management**

   Set realistic and manageable time frames that you need to follow to accomplish your goals. Avoid multi-tasking as it is detrimental to achieving ample focus and concentration. Plan your waking and sleep schedule and follow it religiously. Be sure to enjoy a leisure activity and exercise every other day. There are plenty of free apps that can help you manage your time. If that doesn't work, you can always design a daily schedule with a life coach or therapist.

10. **Goal Setting**

    Set realistic goals that are in line with your life's plan. Strive for balance in your interpersonal relationships (co-workers, friends and family), work, and pleasure-oriented goals. Break up large goals into manageable, bite-sized goals. Don't stress; you will achieve your goals, one step at a time!

Find Relaxation Strategies that Suit You

Imagine that you are at your favorite apparel store, gazing at racks of in-season designer brands. So many choices are available for you to pick the best! Some people love stiletto heels while others love sneakers with a bit of bling. You might choose something similar to an item that you purchased in previous fashion seasons, or you may try a brand new outfit because it calls your name!

In the same manner, there are many options when it comes to relaxation strategies. Find a relaxation plan that works for you. So far, we have spoken about three preferred "brands" of relaxation: **mindfulness, breathing, and Progressive Muscle Relaxation.**

In the Relaxation Strategies section, you were instructed to list some strategies that work for you. Below, we have suggested a list of popular, formal relaxation strategies that have been successfully used by other people. Try some and add those that work to your list!

"Soothing" Activities

- Sounds: ambient music; music you enjoy; "new age," repetitive music; sounds of nature, such as ocean waves or babbling brooks
- Smells (Aromatherapy): incense, candles, etc.
- Sights: Visualization: beaches, falling leaves, etc.
- Nature: hiking, swimming, parks, etc.

"Body-based" Relaxation Strategies

- Slow-paced diaphragmatic breathing
- Yoga
- Progressive Muscle Relaxation and Applied Relaxation
- Massage
- Hot tubs, hot baths, or sauna

"Mind-based" Relaxation Strategies

- Meditation (Mindfulness meditation," Transcendental Meditation, etc.)
- "Body Scan"/body awareness exercises
- Prayer
- Autogenics

Did you know?

Yoga is a well-established, ancient discipline that incorporates a powerful combination of physical and mental elements: stretching, breathing, meditation, and strengthening exercises, aimed at improving psychological and physical well-being. It involves a series of challenging body positions that stretch and strengthen muscles. Yoga is best learned by taking a class with a certified yoga instructor, and it has many benefits, both physical and mental.

In the previous chapters, we introduced some scientific and popular approaches to relaxation that have been utilized successfully by people world-over. It is important to note that the most relaxing activities are those that we enjoy, and which are skillful at doing. In other words, most people enjoy doing what they love because it makes them feel good and because they are good at it. Achieving a sense of accomplishment is important when looking for a practical way to relax. In the next chapter, we will discuss pleasure and mastery, two critical elements of having an enjoyable and relaxed lifestyle.

My Relaxation Plan

Use this worksheet to help you incorporate relaxation into your daily life. Adjust it as you please, be specific, and come up with different strategies. With patience and determination, you will find what works best. Now give it a try!

1. **Formal relaxation exercises (Slow Diaphragmatic Breathing, Yoga, Progressive Muscle Relaxation, Mindfulness):**

   _____

   _____

   _____

   _____

   A. **Practice schedule** (time of day, days per week, etc.):

   _____

   _____

   _____

   _____

2. **Mastery and Pleasure** (things I am good at, socializing, activities I enjoy):

   _____

   _____

   _____

   _____

A. Practice schedule (time of day, days per week, etc.):

_____

_____

_____

_____

3. **Self-care** (read the self-care section and write down ways in which you can improve your life):

_____

_____

_____

_____

A. Practice schedule (time of day, days per week, etc.):

_____

_____

_____

_____

4. **Other soothing activities** (select fun activities from the distraction techniques list):

_____

_____

_____

_____

A. Practice schedule (time of day, days per week, etc.):

_____

_____

_____

_____

5. Are there any lifestyle aspects that increase my stress levels and anxiety on a daily basis? (time management, wok-load, etc.)

_____

_____

_____

_____

A. Practice schedule (time of day, days per week, etc.):

_____

_____

_____

_____

6. What could be modified to reduce stress/anxiety?

_____

_____

_____

_____

A. Practice schedule (time of day, days per week, etc.):

_____

_____

_____

_____

7. How would my life improve if I incorporated some of the elements above into my daily life?

_____

_____

_____

_____

A. Practice schedule (time of day, days per week, etc.):

_____

_____

_____

_____

8. **What can I do today (name one thing), to take the step toward achieving relaxation in my daily life?**

_____

_____

_____

_____

A. Practice schedule (time of day, days per week, etc.):

_____

_____

_____

_____

Relaxation Summary

Relaxation strategies seek to combat anxiety, considering the human body's response to stress.

This booklet discusses **different types of relaxation strategies** and how we can best implement them to alleviate anxiety symptoms.

As is the case with exercising, **long term practice** of relaxation strategies is advised because, in due time, they'll "slow down the mind," slow down the pace of breathing and reduce muscle tension.

In severe cases of anxiety and panic, relaxation strategies might not be powerful enough to reduce the symptoms when they arise. Relaxation skills must be **used in conjunction with the behavioral and cognitive skills** discussed throughout this manual.

CBT and exposure skills work together to **retrain the brain** to have fewer anxiety triggers. Relaxation exercises are not very effective at "retraining" these triggers, which is why they are not typically enough on their own to teach the brain that it can let the "guard" down.

We discussed **breathing skills**; the essential element of breathing is **slowing down the pace of the breath**, which takes practice, considering the nature of anxiety.

Mindfulness techniques were introduced, which aim to "slow down the mind." We learn to see feelings and thoughts for what they are — feelings and thoughts — that move in and out of our subconscious and conscious mind. By entertaining these thoughts without desperately trying to "fix" them, or get rid of them, we communicate more "calm" and less urgency to the body.

Progressive Muscle Relaxation (PMR) involves the tensing and relaxing of muscle groups to better comprehend the difference between tension and relaxation. We can learn to conduct PMR faster through practice and a program called **Applied Relaxation.**

There's something for everyone. Because everyone is different, pick from a selection of formal relaxation strategies, practice them consistently, and **find which relaxation strategy works best**.

Mastery and pleasure activities feel wonderful; therefore, doing more of these activities can only help! The most relaxing activities are the ones that we are good at or enjoy the most. Anxiety causing activities are those activities we don't like or those that are difficult for us to do.

While anxiety can often get in the way of doing fun activities, avoiding pleasurable activities altogether is likely to make the situation worse. It is vital to **incorporate some enjoyable activities** into our daily lives regularly.

Finally, we reviewed crucial elements of **self-care**, such as time management, exercise, and diet. For example, it is difficult to feel relaxed when we are incredibly busy and have not had sufficient rest. By **slowing down** the hectic speed of life, and by taking care of ourselves, we can begin to feel more relaxed.

So Now What?

We have discussed in detail many CBT strategies used to help in coping with anxiety. Use the **Stress Management questionnaire and Anxiety Alleviation workbooks** provided below, manage stress, eliminate anxiety, and regain a stress-free existence!

STRESS MANAGEMENT QUESTIONNAIRE

Stress (definition): Feeling tension or pressure when facing a difficult or challenging situation

What is stress?

• Experiencing stress is a normal part of daily life. It is natural to feel pressure when you pursue goals and take on life's challenges

• Stress is experienced by everyone in a unique and personal way

• Be careful to monitor your stress levels because stress can cause or worsen illness, e.g., hypertension, and for addicts, lead to relapse

• Learn to recognize stress and anxiety (symptoms) in your behavior, thinking, mood, or physical body

• Becoming aware of individual signs of stress is empowering because it allows you to know when to implement stress reduction and relaxation strategies

What are some signs of stress?

Signs of Stress	Check Applicable Box
Anger over minor things	☐
Anxiety	☐
Back pain	☐
Being accident prone	☐
Change in appetite	☐
Dependence on alcohol or drugs	☐
Difficulty falling asleep	☐
Digestion problems	☐
Dry mouth	☐
Feeling restless	☐
Forgetfulness	☐
Headaches	☐
Increased heart rate	☐
Increased need for sleep	☐
Irritability	☐
Problems concentrating	☐
Stomach aches	☐
Sweating	☐
Tearfulness	☐
Trembling or shaking	☐
Other:	☐

What can cause stress?

• Stress is derived from external or internal sources

• Internal stress is usually caused by dwelling on negative thoughts and or placing unreasonable demands on yourself and or by using judgmental self-talk

• External stress is derived from your surrounding environment. It can be caused by daily hassles, and or negative/positive major life events

• Being aware of what triggers stress, helps with preparing in advance and coping in the moment

From the list of stressful events below, which one have you dealt with recently?

Common Causes of Stress	Check Applicable Box
Arguments at home or work	☐
Caring for pets	☐
Crowded living situation	☐
Crowded public transportation	☐
Daily Hassles	☐
Doing business with unpleasant people	☐
Feeling rushed at home or work	☐
Homelessness	☐
Injury or illness of a loved one	☐
Injury, illness, or hospital stay	☐
Job loss or new job	☐
Lack of order or cleanliness at home or work	☐
Legal problems	☐
Life Events	☐
Marriage or divorce	☐
Misplacing things	☐
Money problems or inheriting money	☐
Moving	☐
New baby Long drives or traffic back-ups	☐

New home or work responsibilities	☐
New relationship or break-up	☐
Noise at home or work	☐
Not enough money to spend on leisure	☐
Problems from drug or alcohol use	☐
Stopped smoking or new diet	☐
Unexpected company	☐
Unpleasant chores at home or work	☐
Victim of a crime	☐
Other:	☐

How can I cope with stress?

Just as stress mechanisms and manifestation are unique to every individual, coping with stress is a personal process. Practicing effective coping strategies will help you decrease stress symptoms and enable you to achieve your goals.

Have you used the coping strategies listed below? How has your experience with them been?

Coping Strategy	Already Using	Would like to try using
Balancing activity and rest		
Creating or viewing art		
Listening to music		
Participating in a hobby		
Supporting my spirituality		
Taking care of my health		
Talking or writing about		

my feelings		
Talking to someone		
Using my sense of humor		
Using positive self-talk		
Using relaxation strategies		
Other:		

Therapy Overview

You may use these exercises to help you get started on working on your emotional state. Ultimately, you should engage a therapist who will walk you through these exercises.

ANALYZE A FEARED EVENT

GOALS OF THE EXERCISE

1. Become aware that unnecessary fear and anxiety are irrational emotions
2. Think through the probability of the negative thought happening and its consequences
3. Identify self-talk that is distorted and that mediates the anxiety response
4. Realize that the feared outcome will not prevent you from functioning normally

SUGGESTIONS FOR PROCESSING THIS EXERCISE

Take a bold and objective look at the basis of your anxiety. Acknowledge your fears and comprehend that there are rational alternative outcomes of the feared situations, which will address your fears without devastating your life. Pay attention to distorted cognitions that feed and exacerbate the sense of fear. Counteract fear with realistic and positive self-talk – encourage yourself.

Most of our fears grow in intensity without us stopping to analyze the probability of occurrence, their exact nature, their causes, the amount of control that we might have, and should our fears be realized, the very real outcomes. This exercise will allow you to review your fears thoroughly. As you rationally work through your concerns by analyzing the nature, causes and the real possible outcome of your worries, the fear should dissipate. You will also develop means and methods to cope with stressful situations.

Take this step-by-step approach and look at three of your most common and greatest fears. Present this analysis to your therapist for processing and reinforcement of coping skills.

1. My First Fear

A. What is the anxiety or fear about?

_____

_____

B. On a scale of 1 to 10 (very unlikely to inevitable), what is the possibility of the feared outcome coming to pass?

_____

_____

C. What do you say to yourself during self-talk, that makes the fear grow?

_____

_____

D. If the feared outcome did occur? What are the very real consequences?

_____

_____

E. What steps can you take, to control the feared outcome?

_____

_____

F. If the fear was realized, in your mind, what is the worst possible outcome?

_____

_____

G. How would your life be affected if what you feared happened? How would your normal functioning be affected? What can you do to cope and ensure normal functioning?

_____

_____

2. My Second Fear
    A. What is the anxiety or fear about?

_____

_____

B. On a scale of 1 to 10 (very unlikely to inevitable), what is the possibility of the feared outcome coming to pass?

_____

_____

C. What do you say to yourself during self-talk, that makes the fear grow?

_____

_____

D. If the feared outcome did occur? What are the very real consequences?

_____

_____

E. What steps can you take, to control the feared outcome?

_____

_____

F. If the fear was realized, in your mind, what is the worst possible outcome?

_____

_____

G. How would your life be affected if what you feared happened? How would your normal functioning be affected? What can you do to cope and ensure normal functioning?

_____

_____

3. My Third Fear
    A. What is the anxiety or fear about?

_____

_____

B. On a scale of 1 to 10 (very unlikely to inevitable), what is the possibility of the feared outcome coming to pass?

_____

_____

C. What do you say to yourself during self-talk, that makes the fear grow?

_____

_____

D. If the feared outcome did occur? What are the very real consequences?

_____

_____

E. What steps can you take, to control the feared outcome?

_____

_____

F. If the fear was realized, in your mind, what is the worst possible outcome?

_____

_____

G. How would your life be affected if what you feared happened? How would your normal functioning be affected? What can you do to cope and ensure normal functioning?

_____

_____

FOUR WAYS TO REDUCE FEAR

GOALS OF THE EXERCISE

1. Identify and create specific strategies to resolve fear

2. To minimize the impact of anxiety, implement a particular strategy consistently

3. Increase effectiveness and confidence in coping with the fear

SUGGESTIONS FOR PROCESSING THIS EXERCISE

The focus for this exercise should be in assisting you (the therapy patient), to develop and implement each resolution strategy. Your therapist should offer feedback, direction, and encouragement as needed. If any strategy is deemed ineffective, despite your best efforts, a different option should be selected and implemented.

This exercise will help you to develop four different methods to minimize your fear. On developing the four ways, one will be implemented for a whole week to assist you when you encounter fear. You will rotate the different methods and keep the one that works best.

1. Fully develop each method:

A. **Exaggeration:** Identify your fear; and then imagine it as scary, ugly, big, and so on. Use numerous negative descriptive words, as many as is possible, to describe the fear. Reflect on the most dire consequences imagined.

_____

_____

_____

Application: This exercise allows you to imagine the worst possible outcome so that the things you face don't seem so terrible or humongous

B. **Thought restructuring**: Record three or four of the most common thoughts that you have, which usually leads to an increased sense of fear. On completing that task, ask your therapist to assist you in restructuring your fear-causing thoughts, so as to turn them into realistic and positive thoughts

Thought 1:

_____

_____

Restructured thought:

_____

_____

Thought 2:

_____

_____

Restructured thought:

_____

_____

_____

Thought 3:

_____

_____

Restructured thought:

_____

_____

Thought 4:

_____

_____

Restructured thought:

_____

_____

_____

Application: Our thoughts affect our feelings. By changing our perceptions and beliefs, we change our feelings.

C. **Therapist in your pocket:** Ask your therapist to provide you with four or five statements that will reassure you when encounter any phobia.

Record them commit them to memory. Alternatively, write them on a flash card, and always carry them with you.

1. _____

2. _____

3. _____

4. _____

Application: Encouraging and reassuring statements from people we trust and respect can help us cope with scary or difficult situations.

D. **Relaxing distraction**: Create a relaxing daydream to distract yourself when thinking about or facing the situation you fear. Also choose a relaxing activity to distract at other times (Example: Playing football, sunbathing on the beach)

Daydream:

_____

_____

_____

_____

Activity: (Example: Relaxation breathing, quietly singing

_____

_____

Application: We forget our fears, worries, fears, and troubles when distracted.

2. Choose an approach to fear:

A. Identify which of the above four approaches, i.e., A, B, C or D is most effective in helping you overcome or resolve your fear

B. Explain why you made that choice and why you feel that it would be effective

C. Use an X to indicate your certainty of that approach working for you

|_____|_____|_____|_____|

Very   Sure   Somewhat   A Little   Not at All

On a scale of 1 to 10, rate your determination to overcome your fear.

|_____|_____|

1   5   10

I'll live with it.   I *must* conquer it.

3. Commit to using the approach you choose whenever you encounter any fear over the next week. Evaluate its effectiveness. Replace the approach if not effective.

   1. _____
   2. _____
   3. _____
   4. _____

PAST SUCCESSFUL ANXIETY COPING

GOALS OF THE EXERCISE

1. Identify methods that you used successfully as coping strategies
2. View yourself as a resourceful and capable person who has overcome fear successfully
3. Apply coping strategies from the past that were helpful to help with current anxieties

SUGGESTIONS FOR PROCESSING THIS EXERCISE

This assignment is solution-focused, and it attempts to get you to recognize your past resourcefulness in overcoming and dealing with anxiety. It is sometimes difficult to recognize past resourcefulness, so in conjunction with a therapist, you'll be able to discover the coping mechanisms that have previously helped you. A therapist will also help you clarify and refine the coping skills you used in the past and show you how to apply those skills to your current anxieties. After that, the selected solutions will be monitored and managed as required.

PAST SUCCESSFUL ANXIETY COPING

This assignment encourages you to focus on accomplishments and resources that you have used in your past. We tend to forget our strengths and ability to cope when our fears and anxieties are debilitating and appear to be real. However, most of us, if not all of us, have overcome various life obstacles, fears, and anxiety – we have weathered fierce storms, from childhood to adulthood, and functioned normally in spite of their presence.

For instance, we may have feared showing up to a kindergarten class, but we developed ways to cope, and eventually, that fear was eradicated. We may have feared talking to classmates from the opposite sex, but in spite of our anxiety, we eventually learned to approach and befriend them. We may have feared participating in job interviews, but we pressed forward and managed to present ourselves in the best light possible.

In other words, human beings have the capacity to overcome and function normally, despite anxiety. We cannot allow anxiety to overwhelm us, cripple us, or cause us to avoid circumstances – we must face anxiety boldly. We may have previously coped by taking deep breaths, or through encouraging words from friends, or by frequently rehearsing what we would say or do so that it became second nature. Whatever the case, the coping skills we used successfully in the past must be rediscovered and applied to resolve current anxieties.

A.   Identify three anxieties or fears that you have experienced in the past.

Fear #1:

_____

_____

Fear #2:

_____

_____

Fear #3:

_____

_____

B.   Identify what you did to help you cope, or function normally, in spite of the anxiety.

Fear #1:

_____

_____

Fear #2:

_____

_____

Fear #3:

_____

_____

C.   What makes you feel that the coping mechanism identified above was successful?

Fear #1:

_____

_____

Fear #2:

_____

_____

Fear #3:

_____

_____

D. Mention other coping skills that have helped you in the past to overcome your fears

_____

_____

_____

E. How can you use the coping skills identified in B to help you overcome your current fears?

_____

_____

_____

101 WAYS TO COPE WITH STRESS

INSTRUCTIONS

- Read over the "101 Ways to Cope with Stress" list and circle all the strategies that you already use to cope with stress
- Determine which strategies are most helpful to you and choose one or two to use more frequently as stress reducers during the following week.

101 WAYS TO COPE WITH STRESS

A List of Coping Activities

1. Get up earlier

2. Prepare ahead

3. Avoid tight clothes

4. Avoid chemical aids

5. Set appointments

6. Write it down

7. Practice preventive maintenance

8. Make duplicate keys

9. Say "no" more often

10. Set priorities

11. Avoid negative people

12. Use time wisely

13. Simplify meals

14. Anticipate needs

15. Make repairs

16. Get help with jobs you dislike

17. Break down large tasks

18. Complete difficult and important tasks first

19. Look at problems as challenges

20. Look at challenges differently

21. Unclutter your life

22. Smile

23. Prepare for rain

24. Tickle a baby

25. Pet a dog or cat

26. Don't know all the answers

27. Look for the silver lining

28. Say something nice

29. Teach a kid to fly a kite

30. Walk in the rain

31. Schedule playtime

32. Take a bubble bath

33. Be aware of your decisions

34. Believe in yourself

35. Stop talking negatively

36. Visualize winning

37. Develop a sense of humor

38. Stop thinking tomorrow will be better

39. Have goals

40. Dance a jig

41. Say hello to a stranger

42. Ask a friend for a hug

43. Look at the stars

44. Breathe slowly

45. Whistle a tune

46. Read a poem

47. Listen to a symphony

48. Watch a ballet

49. Read a story

50. Do something new

51. Stop a bad habit

52. Buy a flower

53. Smell a flower

54. Find support

55. Find a "vent partner"

56. Do it today

57. Be optimistic

58. Put safety first

59. Do things in moderation

60. Note your appearance

61. Strive for excellence, not perfection

62. Stretch your limits

63. Enjoy art

64. Hum a jingle

65. Maintain your weight

66. Plant a tree

67. Feed the birds

68. Practice grace

69. Stretch

70. Have a plan

71. Doodle

72. Learn a joke

73. Know your feelings

74. Meet your needs

75. Know your limits

76. Wish people a good day

77. Throw a paper airplane

78. Exercise

79. Learn a new song

80. Go to work earlier

81. Clean a closet

82. Play with a child

83. Go on a picnic

84. Drive a different route to work

85. Leave work early

86. Put air freshener in your car

87. Watch a movie and eat popcorn

88. Write a faraway friend

89. Scream at a ball game

90. Eat a meal by candlelight

91. Recognize the importance of unconditional love

92. Remember that stress is an attitude

93. Keep a journal

94. Share a monster smile

95. Remember your options

96. Build a support network

97. Quit trying to fix others

98. Get enough sleep

99. Talk less and listen more

100. Praise others

101. Relax, take each day as it comes . . . you have one life to live! (YOLO!)

Notes

Made in the USA
San Bernardino, CA
04 August 2020